THE SWEAT OF THE GODS

THE SWEAT OF THE GODS

Myths and Legends of Bicycle Racing

Benjo Maso

Translated by Michiel Horn

THE SWEAT OF THE GODS
Myths and Legends of Bicycle Racing

Benjo Maso

Translated by Michiel Horn

English edition first published in 2005 by
Mousehold Press
Victoria Cottage
Constitution Opening
Norwich, NR3 4BD
www.mousehold-press.co.uk

Originally published in Holland by Atlas under the title
Het zweet der goden

The English edition of this book has been made possible with
financial support from the Foundation for the Production and
Translation of Dutch Literature.

Cover photograph – John Pierce, Photosport International

ISBN 1 874 739 37 4

Printed by Wrightsons Printers, Earls Barton, Northamptonshire

Benjo Maso is a sociologist who has worked in a number of Dutch universities. He has been fascinated by cycle racing since his youth. He is also the author of *We Were All Gods – The Tour de France of 1948*.

Michiel Horn is a Dutch-Canadian historian who remembers some of the exploits of Fausto Coppi, Louison Bobet and Hugo Koblet in their prime.

Introduction

On May 31, 1868, *le tout Paris* gathered in Saint-Cloud Park for a highly unusual spectacle. Instead of the customary horse races, two races were to be held that day on *vélocipèdes*, the new means of transport that had been seen on the streets of the capital since 1861. Although their construction was still extremely primitive, they could nevertheless reach speeds of 25 kilometres per hour. The winner of the first race, one Polocini, completed the course of 1,200 metres in slightly over two-and-a-half minutes. The Englishman James Moore, who won the second race, took approximately the same time. Each man received a gold medal, valued at a hundred francs, awarded by the largest bicycle manufacturer of that time, the Compagnie Parisienne.

Bicycle races had already taken place in the French provinces, but accounts of them had barely reached Paris. The races in Saint-Cloud were, therefore, a complete novelty to those watching them. The spectators were full of admiration for the strength and agility of the participants. The following day the press of the capital city gave extended coverage to the event. From that moment on races quickly succeeded each other, not only in France but also in other European countries.

These races attracted so large a public that the organisers were able to offer substantial prizes in order to attract the best cyclists. Sometimes the winners received 600 francs for their victory, a sum a labourer had to work half a year to earn in those days. Moreover, they also generally got a sizable bonus from the bicycle manufacturers, who used the riders' achievements in advertisements for their machines. In this way the champions of that time could secure a very tidy income. The greatest of them, James Moore, earned so much money from his victories that when his career was over he was able to buy a stud farm in Normandy and a stable of race horses in Chantilly.

Moore became the first cycling star, and so great was his fame that not only his rivals but also his predecessors sank into oblivion. As long as people could remember, Moore had triumphed everywhere and, after some years had passed, public memory did not go back beyond his first victory. It is hardly surprising that the Touring Club of France eventually attached a plaque to a fence at

Saint-Cloud Park: 'On May 31, 1868, James Moore became the winner of the first race for vélocipèdes organised in France.' The statement contains two errors. Even before 1868 bicycle races had been organised in France, and on the day mentioned, James Moore was not the first but the second victor. In the history of cycle sport, fabrications crowded out facts from the very outset. What should have been a monument to the birth of bicycle racing is in reality a monument to its first myth.

The Vélocipède as a good cause

In spite of the success enjoyed by the first races, the bicycle was still a curiosity in 1868. By no means everybody could keep their balance on the contraptions of that time, which weighed 30 kilograms at least. Besides, they were extremely uncomfortable to ride, because their wooden or metal wheels were not yet covered with tyres.

As well as that, physicians pointed to the dangerous consequences of using the new means of transport. In the case of men it allegedly led to impotence, in that of women to infertility. Moreover, the constant friction of the saddle was said to cause a dangerous erotic excitement, a kind of permanent 'sport-engendered masturbation'. Medical authorities claimed that cyclists could often be recognised by their pale and haggard faces. The famous criminologist Cesare Lombroso added that the physical exertion needed to move oneself forward could stimulate criminal and aggressive tendencies. And bicycles were dangerous not only to their riders. Because they weren't equipped with brakes as yet, they were not without risk to others. No wonder they were prohibited in many cities. Even the Bois de Boulogne in Paris was closed to cyclists. At the moment that James Moore scored his first successes, the 'case for the bicycle' had by no means been won, and its opponents were at least as numerous as its defenders.

The keenest supporters of the new means of transport came together in clubs, and even founded periodicals to make their points of view widely known. Two journals, both named *Le Vélocipède*, were established, one in October, 1868, in Foix and the other in March, 1869, in Voiron, near Grenoble. Neither attracted much attention, and both ceased publication after only a few issues had appeared. The Parisian *Le Vélocipède Illustré*, which published its first issue in April, 1869, would enjoy a much longer life. It owed its success mostly to the activist policy of its editors, who were able to gain a much larger readership than their rivals by means of a daring initiative: in 1869 they decided to organise a bicycle race on the open road, a 135-kilometre race from Paris to Rouen. According to the journal's management, an event of this kind was the best way to remove doubts about the possibilities of the bicycle once and for all:

> To win adherents to the good cause of the vélocipède, it must be shown that the bicycle allows riders to cover considerable distances at the cost of far less fatigue than if they had walked. Faced with established facts, the public will take note of the genuine merits of the vélocipède, from which one can confidently expect savings in both time and effort.

It is possible that the editors were driven by purely idealistic motives, although they did not neglect to mention that one could wager on the outcome. But they must soon have realised that their fervour on behalf of the good cause had an extraordinarily agreeable side effect: sales of *Le Vélocipède Illustré* rose by leaps and bounds. Races like the one in Saint-Cloud Park were rarely longer than five kilometres, and the public showed themselves to be keenly interested in the question of what would happen during a 'monster race' of more than a hundred kilometres. Nobody had the faintest idea, the organisers included. They found it necessary, for example, to state in the rules and regulations that cyclists could not be accompanied by their dogs. And, because few people can resist the temptation to express opinions about an issue that everyone is ignorant about, the columns of the organising journal were filled for weeks with the most detailed prognoses and counsels. In this spirit, a physician advised the cyclists to pause every 20 to 25 kilometres for food and drink, preferably a steak accompanied by a couple of glasses of Madeira or sweet white wine. Then, after fifteen minutes' rest, it was advisable to walk alongside one's bicycle for a few minutes before getting back on.

Not only the public, but cyclists also showed great interest. *Le Vélocipède Illustré* received more than two hundred entries. They came from a very mixed bag of people, including men and women – women's bicycle racing is as old as men's –, amateurs and professionals, tricycle- as well as bicycle-riders, circus acrobats and members of the aristocracy (who mostly entered under pseudonyms). Some objected to the participation of professional racing cyclists, a category that had been officially established as early as 1868, but the editors did not yield to these complaints. After all, the best French riders rode for money, and if they were not allowed to appear at the start there would be too great a danger of a foreign victory. Moreover, the organisers believed that it was far from certain that the short-course champions would be strongest over a long distance. In this respect the bicycle manufacturers were more realistic, and they paid large amounts for the privilege of supplying the well-known professionals with equipment. The public, likewise, lacked much faith in unknown amateurs, and three-quarters of the wagers accepted by bookmakers were placed on the 'unbeatable' James Moore.

Moore did indeed win, and claimed first prize – a thousand gold francs put up by the Compagnie Parisienne. Unfortunately for this company, he was riding a bicycle made by a competitor, Jean Suriray, which naturally did not neglect to make the success of its machine known far and wide by means of posters and advertisements in the major newspapers. The manufacturers who had supplied the other prize-winners also placed ads in *Le Vélocipède Illustré* praising the quality of their products.

All parties involved in the organisation of the Paris–Rouen race had reason to be pleased. The editors of *Le Vélocipède Illustré* saw a marked rise in their journal's circulation; the manufacturers used the widespread interest in the race to advertise their bicycles; and the winner earned a sum of money for which a school teacher would have had to put in a full year's work. In this way Paris–Rouen demonstrated for the first time that perfect symbiosis of the media, commerce, and riders which still constitutes the basis of the sport of bicycle racing.

Although each of the three interested parties was able to profit from the race, none of them fully realised as yet how they could optimally exploit their opportunities. For example, the manufacturers supplied the best possible equipment, but did not yet seek to support their riders in other ways. The cyclists had no tactical sense and from the start launched a continuing assault on the leading positions. Because most were unable to ration their strength effectively, many spectacular collapses occurred: several riders were not even able to complete the race despite having been among the leaders 25 kilometres before the finish. Finally, newspapers had little clue about how to give a gripping account of a bicycle race. The *Petit Parisien* published the following article:

Of the many cyclists who left Paris on Sunday morning to go to Rouen, Mr James Moore arrived as first, at 6:10 p.m. Thus he covered the distance of more than 130 kilometers in 10 hours and 40 minutes. Mr Moore did not seem tired. The cyclists arriving after him were, in order, Messrs A. Castéra, J. Bobillier, H. Pascaud, G. Biot, B. Cantellauve, A. Johnson and J. Meunier.

The story in Le Vélocipède Illustré was a good deal longer, of course, but its tone was to all intents and purposes the same. Its journalists tried to give as detailed an account of events as possible, so that what they wrote sounded a bit like the minutes of a meeting.

This desiccated style did not detract from the success of the race: the public was interested in the event itself, not in the way in which it was described. Readers were so fascinated that the editors of Le Vélocipède Illustré immediately resolved to organise a second edition. The race had been held in the pouring rain, and it would be interesting, they wrote, to see how the event would proceed under different conditions, in sunshine or in snow.

All these plans came to nought. Twenty-seven years would go by before Paris–Rouen took place again. This was not just because of the outbreak of war between France and Prussia in July 1870, which temporarily put an end to all sporting events; other major road races of the time usually took place only once. In fact, bicycle racing was almost wholly relocated to velodromes. These were mostly improvised tracks, but England, in particular, saw the construction of velodromes with high banked corners where considerable speeds could be reached. The great advantage of track-racing was that spectators could follow the action from beginning to end. This allowed organisers to charge the public an entrance fee which, given sufficient interest, could generate big profits. Two of the leading riders of the time, the Waller brothers, travelled all over England with a portable mini-track in a kind of circus tent, and earned a fortune.

Initially the sports journals performed an important role in organising track-races. Because it was naturally to their advantage to spread the news about these races over as many days as possible, a British journalist, Harry Etherington, hit on the idea of holding a race that would last from Monday morning to Saturday evening – in those days the British Sunday was still sacrosanct. Whoever had covered the greatest distance in that time would be the winner. This six-day race not only attracted a large audience but also gave Etherington a week-long opportunity to publish special issues containing the latest news about the riders' positions.

Races of this kind drew considerably more attention from cycling fans than the major road races. These continued to arouse public enthusiasm only when there were impressive individual performances; the race aspect was less important. For this reason there was little point in holding more than one race over the same route. At that time road racing was a bit like mountain climbing: the first time a peak is scaled makes major news; the second time attracts the attention only of insiders.

To interest the public, the organisers of road races were forced to keep looking for longer and more exciting courses. The problem with this was that the limits were soon reached. Riders were still riding hard-to-manage high bicycles with wheels that were shod with a strip of solid rubber at best. Given that the roads were largely unpaved at that time, 250 kilometres seemed to be the maximum distance that could be completed on such vehicles. This limit was passed only after the bicycle had undergone important improvements. The high vélocipèdes had to make way for bicyclettes on which the pedals were no longer attached to the front wheel but drove the rear wheel by means of a chain. In 1888 the Scottish veterinary surgeon, John Boyd Dunlop, developed the first pneumatic tyre, which made cycling noticeably faster and more comfortable. In 1889 the Englishman George Pilkington Mills, using the new model bicycle, succeeded in completing 475 kilometres in 24 hours. When the biggest French cycling journal, *Véloce-Sport*, merged with a rival and moved its head office from Paris to Bordeaux, its editors sought to give maximum publicity to this event. They did not hesitate to announce a race between these two cities, a distance of 575 kilometres, 'more demanding and unforgiving than the 24-hour races organised by the British'.

To add lustre to their race, the organisers sought to secure the participation of British cyclists, who had the reputation of being the strongest in the world. The only problem was that they were amateurs, that is to say 'gentlemen', and did not want to compete against professionals, 'working-class' men. The organisers yielded to their demands, even though this meant that the best French riders were not allowed to enter. The result was that the first four places were taken by cyclists from the United Kingdom, much to the chagrin of the viewing public.

The victory by the British riders was due not only to their athletic abilities. At least as important was the support they received from their 'sponsors'. The English bicycle manufacturers were highly conscious of the publicity value of a victory in the longest road race ever held. For that reason they left no stone unturned to give riders who were using their bicycles every advantage. For example, they retained the French champion, Charles Terront, and other well-known professionals who had not been allowed to participate in the race, to accompany the British amateurs and shield them from the wind – a practice permitted by the rules. The French manufacturers had no answer to this. In the early years of the vélocipède they had a big lead on their competitors in other countries, but during the war with Prussia in 1870-71 they largely stagnated. Besides, the victors saddled France with such a huge sum in reparations that in the first years after peace was signed not much money was available for new investment. The result was that the French companies were completely overtaken by the British bicycle industry. Moreover, they did not have at their disposal the finance to hire such good pacemakers as those used by their British rivals. These very naturally made ample use of their victory in Bordeaux–Paris to strengthen their position even further. The Humber Company distributed a large number of posters and advertisements on both sides of the English Channel, citing George Pilkington Mills's first place as evidence of the superiority of its products.

Public interest in Bordeaux–Paris was so enormous that the non-specialised press, which so far had paid virtually no attention to bicycle races, began to show an interest for the first time. Pierre Giffard, editor of *Le Petit Journal*, the biggest newspaper in France with a circulation of one million, decided at once to take advantage of the mounting popularity of cycle sport by organising a race that would put Bordeaux–Paris completely in the shade. Two weeks after Mills's victory, Giffard announced a race from Paris to Brest and back, a distance of 1,200 kilometres. He did not mean to make the same mistake as the editors of *Véloce-Sport*, who in their race had offered victory on a platter to the British riders. Bordeaux–Paris had been a test of brute force, he wrote. But more would be needed for a victory in Paris–Brest–Paris: intelligence, wisdom, cautiousness, and skill. In other words, it would be a typically French race, and therefore it went almost without saying that only Frenchmen would be allowed to enter. They would have to complete the whole distance on the same bicycle, to demonstrate thereby the awe-inspiring possibilities of this new means of transport: not just useful and healthy but with the potential of becoming an essential part of national defence. It was not unthinkable that a courageous bicycle raid might some day save *la patrie*.

Giffard's announcement aroused tremendous excitement. Many had been convinced that the limits of human endurance had been reached with the 575 kilometres of Bordeaux–Paris, and competing journals hastened to characterise Giffard's initiative as a cheap publicity stunt. The most bitter comments could be found in the cycling papers *Véloce-Sport* and *La Bicyclette*, whose editors found it hard to swallow that a major national daily was encroaching on territory where they had hitherto enjoyed sole rights.

The hope of some commentators that no one would be crazy enough to enter the race went unfulfilled. On the contrary, within a few weeks hundreds of entries had come into the offices of *Le Petit Journal*. Some of these potential participants had never been on a bicycle before, but felt so inspired by Giffard's patriotic challenge that they had begun to take lessons solely for the purpose of being able to join the race. All the same, their entries were accepted. Giffard actually wrote that it was altogether possible that victory would go to a complete unknown, a Sunday cyclist with better understanding and more stamina than the trained athletes.

Of course this was an illusion. In fact, there were only four serious contenders: Jules Dubois, Henri Coullibeuf, Charles Terront, and Jacques Jiel-Laval. Not only were they among the best racing cyclists at that time, but they were the only participants with teams of pacemakers at their disposal. Of course they did not pay for these out of their own pocket: the costs were borne by the manufacturers who had supplied them with their equipment.

Jiel-Laval was riding on a French Clément bicycle equipped with Dunlop tyres. Terront had secured the support of the mighty Humber Company and was also using a new invention by the Michelin brothers from Clermont-Ferrand: pneumatic tyres that were removable and hence could be repaired unusually quickly – within half an hour. His opponents gave him ample opportunity to test its value, because Terront encountered a remarkably large number of brand new tacks and nails in his path. He himself used ruses, too. For example, he had sent a spy up ahead to report when Jiel-Laval, who was far in the lead, was taking a break. When the latter disappeared into a café to take a brief nap, Terront made a detour, so that four hours went by before it finally dawned on Clément's manager, posted outside the café to keep an eye out, that he had been tricked. From that moment the race was all but over. Once Terront had no more cyclists ahead of him his tyres stayed undamaged, and after almost three full days he reached Paris with a lead of seven hours and 40 minutes on Jiel-Laval, and more than 24 hours on the rest of his rivals. Almost a week passed before the last of the nearly one hundred cyclists who completed the race reached the finish line.

During the three days that the race lasted, something of the same cycling fever held sway in France as would be observed later during the Tour de France. *Le Petit Journal* published several extra editions daily to report the passage of the leaders past the control points. Tens of thousands of Parisians turned out to witness Terront's arrival. All at once he became the most famous man in France. Eighteen banquets were organised in his honour, he got a free box in the Paris Opera, his memoirs became a best-seller, and he entered literature as Serront in Paul d'Ivoi's novel *Les cinq sous de Lavarède*. His reputation was so huge that organisers of track races paid him appearance fees of 2,500 francs and more.

What astonished the public above all was that Terront had cycled for three days and three nights without sleeping. But this was not all that extraordinary. In six-day races over in England, still completed by individuals and not by teams of two, riders were making ample use of medications containing caffeine and other stimulants in order to stay awake. Terront, one of a few French riders who regularly crossed the English Channel to participate in these six-day races, was no doubt well aware of this, in contrast with the hapless Jiel-Laval, who was still an amateur. And it stands to reason that Terront used these magic potions, which were not banned at the time. In any case, it speaks volumes that after the race ended a full day went by before he was able to get to sleep.

Paris–Brest–Paris had been so unspeakably difficult that most of the participants announced they would certainly not enter a second race over a distance like that. None of the heroes of *Le Petit Journal*'s monster race, Terront, Jiel-Laval and the others, appeared at the start of Paris-Nantes-Rennes-Paris, a 1,025-kilometre race organised by the *Revue des Sports*. The editors of competing cycling journals, who were also dreaming of races that would last for days, therefore had to limit their ambitions.

Fortunately it was no longer necessary to demand superhuman performances from the riders. After Paris–Brest–Paris the popularity of cycling had grown so much that races over shorter distances were also followed with great excitement. Interest in track races increased spectacularly as well, especially when the heroes of the open road appeared at the start. Everywhere the improvised tracks of the early days gave way to velodromes with huge stands, not just in France but in other countries too. Above all, challenge races held over long distances drew a big public. For example, more than 20,000 spectators watched Terront and Jean-Marie Corre fight a 2,500-lap duel, totalling 1,000 kilometres, on the winter track of the Galerie des machines in Paris. Terront won, and with his victory earned a prize of no less than 12,500 francs. Bicycle racing became such a craze that Clovis Clère, manager of the Folies-Bergères, not only built a velodrome in Charenton, but held races on rollers in his nightclub.

x x x

Of course, the cycling journals profited from the mounting popularity of the sport as well, and achieved unprecedented circulation levels. This led Pierre Giffard to leave *Le Petit Journal* in 1893 and launch a sports journal, *Le Vélo*, that would appear not once or twice a week like the competition, but every day. This paper soon captured the larger part of the reading market, especially after Giffard succeeded in taking over the organisation of Bordeaux–Paris, the most popular race of the cycling season, from *Véloce-Sport*. The surest way for cycling journals to increase circulation at least temporarily was to organise road races. As organisers, they quite naturally assumed a privileged position and thus were very largely able to monopolise information about the course of the race. For this reason the sports press kept holding new races. Most of them had just one edition. Others were destined to have a longer life, and a few survive to this day, such as Paris–Roubaix and Paris–Tours, both run for the first time in 1896 under the auspices of *Paris-Vélo*, and Paris–Brussels, organised by *La Bicyclette* and dating back to 1893.

Because of the great interest in these races they served the manufacturers as a superior method of advertising their bicycles. In part due to the spectacular fashion in which Terront had demonstrated the bicycle's possibilities in Paris–Brest–Paris, sales of bicycles rose enormously in spite of the high prices they continued to command. In 1890 the number of bicycle owners in France was still below 30,000. In 1893 this number had risen to 130,000, four years later to 375,000, and yet another four years later to a million. In order to secure the largest possible share of this expanding market, manufacturers were willing to engage the principal champions for big sums of money. In 1893 the Clincher tyre company offered Terront 10,000 francs to cycle from St. Petersburg to Paris; to this amount the English bicycle builder Daniel Rudge added 2,000 francs. Earlier that year, the two enterprises had joined in paying Terront 5,000 francs for a track race of 1,000 kilometres. During the major road races, manufacturers spent huge amounts to provide their riders with strong pacemakers and to take good care of them. For example, in 1897 the Gladiator company was prepared to invest 60,000 guilders in the first Dutch cycling star, Matieu Cordang, who entered the Bordeaux–Paris and Paris–Roubaix races that year.

It hardly needs saying that few manufacturers could afford such expenditure. The intervention by commercial firms was also in complete conflict with the ideal that Pierre de Coubertin was promulgating at the time, namely that a race must be an unadulterated test of strength between athletes. Cyclists who rode as individuals, or for small teams, had virtually no chance of winning. Because of the enormous stakes, managers were often willing to protect their investments by all possible means, both legal and illegal. In spite of the attempts by organisers to guarantee a fair and clean race, many instances of bribery and cheating took place.

x x x

How little value the manufacturers attached to the sporting aspects of bicycle racing is clear from the events they organised themselves, such as the Course Michelin in 1892, a 400-kilometre race between Paris and Clermont-Ferrand. The impetus for this race came from a new invention by the Michelin brothers, the replaceable inner tube. This could be repaired within five minutes, while mending the removable pneumatic tubes that Terront had used for Paris–Brest–

Paris the year before took almost half an hour. To make sure there would be enough punctured tyres for the benefits of the new system to be clearly shown, the organisers dumped 25 kilos of tacks on the part of the course that had to be completed at night. The eighteen-year old Englishman Henry Farman, the fastest rider using Michelin tyres, was declared to be the winner. Yet he was not the first to cross the finish line. That honour went to Auguste Stéphane, who used Dunlop tyres. He had been immediately disqualified, because along the way he had changed bikes several times, something prohibited by the regulations. Stéphane made no secret of this, and of course he knew very well that he could not claim victory, but that did not matter. The only purpose of his participation in the race was to enable his tyre factory to keep the publicity battle with the Michelin brothers going. After the race, Dunlop's French representatives placed large advertisements claiming that 'the outcome of Paris-Clermont-Ferrand offered one more piece of evidence of the great superiority of Dunlop tyres'. Whereupon the Michelins felt themselves compelled to pay for special inserts in the sports papers in order to issue a detailed refutation of their rival's claims.

In spite of the shady methods occasionally used by organisers and manufacturers, in the early 1890s it seemed that nothing could disturb the popularity of cycle sport. Interest in the races held on track and road was so great that the public simply put up with the less attractive aspects of the sport. But when, by the end of the decade, bicycle racing found itself facing ever increasing competition from other sports, these weaknesses threatened to become fatal. Riders and journalists did not yet know how they could reliably hold the interest of the public. The only group which knew how to utilise the possibilities of the sport to the full were the manufacturers. Unfortunately, their contribution largely undermined the sporting spectacle.

Around 1900 the public which had filled the stands of the velodromes were increasingly migrating to football and rugby matches that offered a much more exciting show than long-distance track racing, in which hours went by without anything of significance taking place. Only the sprints continued to attract large numbers of spectators, especially when some American star engaged a local favourite in battle. On other occasions the turnout was often so low that many cycling tracks were finally closed down. Even the famous Buffalo Velodrome in Paris was torn down in 1901. In

Belgium and Germany, interest declined so steeply at this time that national track championships were no longer even held.

Road racing, which could only be followed through the press and not from the stands, suffered less than track racing from the rise of football and rugby. But as a result of the invention of the motor car and the arrival of motor sport it, too, threatened to slip in rank. Bicycle manufacturers such as Humber and Triumph, which had played an important role in cycle sport as race sponsors, were concentrating more and more on the construction of motor cars. Some racing cyclists made the same switch and became racing-car drivers, among them Farman and Albert Champion (the winner of Paris–Roubaix in 1899), who would later become a famous sparkplug manufacturer. What is more, readers of the sports papers showed an increasing interest in car races, driven at ever greater speeds and therefore offering something new every time. In the eyes of many they inspired much more gripping prose than the major bicycle races, which had been run according to the same formula for years. To be sure, the re-run of Paris–Brest–Paris in 1901 aroused a lot of interest, but not as much as the first running of the motor race from Paris to Berlin that year. The interest in motor races became so great that the new sports daily founded in 1900 was named *L'Auto-Vélo*. When a court found for the management of its competitor *Le Vélo*, who had objected to the name of the new paper, its editor-in-chief, Henri Desgrange, simply changed it to *L'Auto*.

Bicycle racing, which had monopolised the interest of sports fans for almost 30 years, was in danger of dropping from public sight. But in the very year that Desgrange removed the word 'Vélo' from the name of his newspaper, he would give cycle sport a stimulus that raised its popularity higher than ever: he announced a stage-race that would take the participating cyclists through all of France, the Tour de France.

2

A Sports Epic

The genesis of the Tour de France is encrusted with so many myths that the truth can scarcely be recovered, all the more so because the archives of the journal that organised it were lost during the Second World War. It all starts with the establishment of *L'Auto-Vélo*, which after 1903 was simply called *L'Auto*. The story goes that Pierre Giffard, editor-in-chief of *Le Vélo*, with a circulation of 80,000 by far the biggest sports paper of that time, had chosen the side of the unfortunate Captain Alfred Dreyfus, and that this motivated a group of rich anti-Dreyfusards to start publishing their own sports journal. Up to a point this story is undoubtedly true. Giffard's attitude during the Dreyfus Affair had indeed earned him the enmity of the motor car manufacturer Count Philippe Albert de Dion, who became the president of the new journal. But the first issue of *L'Auto-Vélo* appeared in October, 1900, a year after Dreyfus had been freed. Moreover, Henri Desgrange, editor-in-chief of the new publication, announced at the outset that there would be no space in the columns of his paper for pronouncements about the affair: 'There will never be room for political issues in *L'Auto-Vélo*. Readers, be for or against you know what, but don't ever expect *L'Auto-Vélo* to express an opinion about it.' On top of that, Desgrange was in no way fervently anti-Dreyfusard. The article with which, on 1 July 1903, he announced the start of the Tour de France opened with a favourable reference to Dreyfus's most famous defender, Émile Zola.

In fact, it is far more likely that the founding of *L'Auto-Vélo* was inspired primarily by commercial motives. The largest shareholders in the new journal were prominent figures from the industrial sector: the car-makers Dion, Baron Etienne de Zuylen de Nyevelt, and Count Gaston de Chasseloup-Laubat; the bicycle manufacturer Adolphe Clément; and Edmond Michelin, co-owner of the famous tyre company. In those days the sports press constituted an important publicity medium for the industry, and its representatives were naturally little pleased with *Le Vélo*'s dominant position, which enabled Giffard to charge high advertising rates and to use the editorial columns for the distribution of favours as he saw fit. With their new initiative, the industrialists tried to provide a serious rival to Giffard in the hope of breaking his power.

Henri Desgrange, who after a brief career as an amateur racing cyclist had been publicity manager for Clément for a couple of years, did what was expected from him. He succeeded in 1901 in persuading *Le Petit Journal* to entrust him with the organisation of the second running of Paris–Brest–Paris, originally a creation of Giffard's! The next year he held his own Bordeaux–Paris fixture in order to diminish the lustre of the version organised by *Le Vélo* earlier that year. Moreover, he created a monster race of his own: Marseilles–Paris, a distance of 800 kilometres. All these initiatives were tactical master strokes, but they yielded only a modest return. At the end of 1902, *L'Auto-Vélo*'s circulation reached 30,000, which was reasonably good for a recently-launched journal but looked pretty thin alongside the 80,000 *Le Vélo* could boast.

The legal judgment of 15 January 1903, which forced the management of *L'Auto-Vélo* to alter the paper's name on grounds of 'plagiarism', was a new blow. Circulation sagged to 20,000, and it was no accident that, four days later, Desgrange decided to announce his plan for a cycling tour through all of France. Not that he expected much from the initiative. As the name of the new journal implied, Desgrange believed that the future belonged to motor-sport and not to cycle sport. During the months after his announcement, he paid far more attention to the motor race from Madrid to Paris, held on 25 May, than to his own Tour de France. The news coverage of this event he assigned largely to his assistant, Géo Lefèvre, the man who had first conceived the idea of organising a Tour through France.

The Tour was announced with a lot of fanfare, but most of the cycling champions showed so little enthusiasm for *L'Auto*'s proposal that hardly any entries came in during the first few months. The six stages of approximately 400 kilometres each would be completed at the rate of one per week, which meant that the participants would be away from home for well over a month. Furthermore, Desgrange had decided to allow pacemakers on the last day only, because the manufacturers would otherwise be faced with costs that were too high. This meant that the riders would have to cover almost 2,000 kilometres under their own steam. Finally, the prize money was a sad illustration of the decline that cycle sport was undergoing at the time: the total purse was only 20,000 francs, of which 3,000 would go to the leader in the final overall classification. This was actually less than the amount Terront had occasionally received for just one race. Only after the editorial board had improved the financial conditions and had limited the number of rest days so that the race would last a total of nineteen days, did enough entries come in to make the event feasible. All the same, Desgrange had so little faith in the success of the race that he decided not to put his own prestige on the line, and to leave direction of the Tour to Géo Lefèvre.

Initially Desgrange's pessimism seemed justified. Only a few hundred enthusiasts showed up to watch the start of the Tour. Desgrange made noticeably less room on L'Auto's front page for the finish of the first stage than he did for racing-car driver René de Knyff, who looked to have a good chance of victory in the Gordon Bennett Trophy, to be run on 2 July. But as the Tour progressed, the headlines grew in size. The results of the fourth stage were spread over the whole width of the front page, even though most of it was filled with comment about the sprint duels between the popular Edmund Jacquelin and 'the Flying Negro', the American cyclist Marshall 'Major' Taylor. Three days later the sprinters had been moved onto the inside pages. And upon the completion of the last stage, news about the Tour occupied the entire front page.

The reason for this development was that the attitude of the public had changed radically during the course of the Tour. The accounts telegraphed to Paris by Lefèvre and his colleagues aroused so much interest that during the concluding stages there was little left of the initial indifference. The circulation of L'Auto rose from 20,000 to 65,000, and tens of thousands of Parisians turned out to witness the arrival of the surviving riders. In honour of the winner, Maurice Garin, a series of banquets was organised just as for Terront twelve years earlier. The butcher's apprentice Lucien Pothier, who came in second, received a gold medal from the Butchers' Sports Association, and other riders who had distinguished themselves were welcomed as heroes in their home towns.

The Tour engendered so much enthusiasm that the next year the public began to interfere actively with the course of the race. Spectators sprinkled dozens of kilos of carpet tacks, thumb tacks, caltrops, and broken glass on the roads. Stage finishes occasionally deteriorated into fully-fledged battles. Near Saint-Etienne the riders in the leading group were attacked by supporters of the local favourite, Antoine Faure, and beaten with clubs, so that they had to be rescued by the race director, a pistol-firing Géo Lefèvre. In Nîmes a mob of cycling fans from the neighbouring town of Alais tried to lynch two riders – Philippe Jousselin and Hyppolite Aucouturier – in protest against the disqualification of their fellow townsman Ferdinand Payan, who had used a car to pull him along.

Payan was not the only one guilty of irregularities. In the first year the riders did not yet know exactly what to expect, but by 1904 they were better prepared. Many had supplied themselves with railway schedules and ordnance survey maps, on which they had carefully noted the opportunities for shortcuts. The roads along which the Tour de France was run were not yet blocked off, so that every cyclist or motorist had the right to join the peloton. Moreover, because the stages were partly ridden by night, the possibilities for fraud were almost endless. Spectators swore they had seen riders allowing themselves to be towed by cars by means of steel wires attached to corks that they held in their mouths. To maintain the appearance of a sportsmanlike race, Lefèvre and Desgrange initially levied high fines for relatively small offences – at least that is how they were described in *L'Auto*. Later on, two riders were actually disqualified. This brought Desgrange into conflict with the French Cycling Federation, which according to the regulations was the only body empowered to impose such a penalty. The federation refused to accept the Tour results and decided a few months later to disqualify the first four in the final standings. The result was that the victory of the nineteen-year old Henri Cornet, who had escaped with a reprimand, had scarcely any value. No wonder that Desgrange saw little benefit in continuing his enterprise. 'The Tour de France is over,' he wrote, 'and I fear its second edition will have been the last. It has died from its own success, from the passions it has unchained.' Desgrange concluded his article with the words: 'For the time being we shall leave to others the cares of dealing with adventures similar to the Tour de France, while we examine what other kinds of possibilities exist for next year.'

Unfortunately there were few other possibilities. The motor sport that was so close to Desgrange's heart had sustained far greater blows than the Tour. The race from Paris to Madrid, which had been announced as the high point of 1903, had to be abandoned halfway through after a series of fatal accidents. The organisers had anticipated there would be victims but thought their number would be limited to three or four. And according to Desgrange, who as an admirer of Napoleon evidently honoured the Emperor's dictum that you can't make an omelet without breaking eggs, this was an 'acceptable maximum, a small price to pay for the progress of so important an industry as motor car manufacturing'. But by the time the riders, among them the ex-racing cyclist Henry Farman and the car makers Louis Renault, Ettore Bugatti, and Charles Stewart Rolls, reached Bordeaux, this 'maximum' had already been far exceeded. The authorities prohibited the continuation of the race. With this came an end to the popular races between the European capitals that had given an important stimulus to the sales of L'Auto.

Desgrange therefore had little choice but to give the Tour another chance. He did decide to take a number of measures that would serve to reduce irregularities as much as possible. He expanded the number of stages but reduced their length, so that the riders would have to complete the greater part of them in full daylight. To prevent the chaotic scenes at the finish lines, he thought of a highly original method – one which emphasised, by the way, that road races were organised for riders rather than spectators: the place where the finish line was drawn would be kept secret. In part because of these measures, the Tour became a success. Many serious incidents still occurred during the early stages, but there were few grounds for criticism of the remaining part. The interest of the public was even greater than during the first two editions, and the circulation of L'Auto passed the 100,000 mark. The idea of holding a stage-race through all of France had initially appealed to Desgrange, above all, as a way of breaking through the barriers that seemed to have been reached with the monster races. The Tour added up to twice as many kilometres as Paris–Brest–Paris and thereby became the longest cycling race in the world. The success of the Tour confirmed Desgrange in his conviction that heroic feats were the best way of arousing the public's interest. To make them possible he kept looking for new ways of making the route of the Tour longer and more difficult.

With this in mind, Desgrange announced in 1905 that, for the first time, he would include mountains in his Tour, namely the Ballon d'Alsace, the Côte de Laffrey, and the Col Bayard. Two years later he expanded the number of ascents with a stage through the Chartreuse Massif. The Pyrenees followed in 1910, the Galibier in the French Alps east of Grenoble in 1911. With its height of 2,556 metres, this would for some time to come be the highest French col that could be ascended by bicycle, so that a temporary limit had been reached. Even after this, though, public enthusiasm for the Tour kept on growing. The reason was that Desgrange and his assistants had developed not only a new race formula but also a new kind of sports journalism. The accounts of Bordeaux–Paris or Paris–Roubaix were short stories; the reportage about the Tour made up a serial, which the writers provided with all the classic features belonging to the genre.

From Paris–Rouen on, cycling journalists had done their best to reconstruct the course of the race as faithfully as possible. This meant that their accounts aroused interest only when the races they wrote about provided sufficient excitement. Therefore the organising journals saw themselves forced to keep finding newer, even more sensational courses. As the editors of L'Auto discovered, more or less by accident, this was quite unnecessary. What grips the readers of sports journals is not the progress of the race itself, but the manner in which it is described. Evert Straat, for years the chess columnist of De Volkskrant, said once that the chief model for every sports journalist ought to be Homer: a poet who knew how to turn a fight between two bands of robbers over a slut into an immortal epic.

First among L'Auto's editors to put this insight into practice was Géo Lefèvre. The Tour was his baby. He was the first to have broached the idea of a Tour, and at first he not only looked after the organisation but also took care of the reporting of the event. In the spring of 1903 it looked as if his initiative would turn into a fiasco, because none of the big stars seemed to be planning to take a chance on the adventure. Lefèvre therefore decided to create new stars. Cyclists like Hyppolite Pagie, Alexandre Foureaux, and Lucien Pothier, none of whom had won a race up to that point, were given Homeric epithets such as 'the Prince of Mines', 'the Carpenter Champion' and 'the terrible butcher from Lens'. Lefèvre lavished special attention on Jean Dargassies, 'the burly blacksmith from Grisolles', who had never taken part in a race but to make up for this had cycled from his village in the Languedoc to Paris. News about the heroic deeds of Dargassies, who rode an excellent Tour and finished eleventh, became a daily motif in the accounts Lefèvre sent to Paris.

Desgrange, who began to concern himself ever more actively with the reporting as the success of the Tour became clearer, adopted

Lefèvre's approach and was able to intensify it. Thus after the conclusion of the final stage he did not write that 'Messrs Garin, Pothier and Augereau did not seem tired,' as his predecessors would have done, but embellished his account with phrases such as these:

> The steepest mountains, the coldest and blackest nights, the sharpest and most violent winds, constant and unjust reverses, the most difficult routes, never-ending slopes and roads that just keep going on and on – nothing has been able to break the determination and willpower of these men.

With bombastic prose of this kind, Desgrange became the principal architect of the myth of 'the giants of the road', an expression he first used on the eve of the Tour's arrival in Paris. In his descriptions, races always proceeded far more heroically, dramatically and sportingly than could possibly have been the case in reality. Information that detracted from this picture was kept out of *L'Auto*'s columns as much as possible. Responsibility for the nails and tacks that were constantly being sprinkled on the roads he ascribed to 'vandals' and 'thugs', even though he was well aware that some riders used this method to hurt the chances of their rivals. The German rider, Hans Ludwig, who wrote a booklet in 1913 containing tips for would-be colleagues, stated, for example, that the cyclists of his day never neglected to bring a small bag of nails along. These had a weighted round head, so that the sharp end was always upwards when they were thrown upon the ground. When the organisers of major races moved to checking the luggage of participants, the riders hid the nails in their water bottles or handlebars.

Typical of the way in which Desgrange and his assistants sought to give their race a heroic aspect is the manner in which mountain stages were introduced in 1905. Desgrange represented these as an unprecedented and dangerous experiment whose outcome no one could predict. About the first mountain that had to be climbed that year he wrote: 'None of us knows what the Ballon d'Alsace will bring. The passage through the mountains is this year's great novelty. Our fear matches that of the riders.' In his account of the ascent he once again emphasised the unique character of the occasion:

The five riders at the front waged a battle that without the slightest exaggeration I can characterise as a sporting epic ... It was splendid, it was gripping. The ascent of the Ballon d'Alsace is one of the most exciting events I have ever witnessed and confirms for the umpteenth time that human courage knows no limits and that a well-trained athlete is capable of the most incredible achievements.

Whatever Desgrange might claim, though, mountain ascents in bicycle races were nothing new. There is a tiny chance that Desgrange was uninformed about the race over the Brenner Pass in 1894, but it can hardly have escaped him that riders in the 1903 and 1904 Tours had to conquer a genuine mountain, the Col de la République, which at 1,161 metres was a mere seventeen metres lower than the Ballon. At the time Desgrange paid no special attention to it; the concept of the Tour was so new that he did not yet recognise the rhetorical possibilities of an ascent. When he made up for this omission in 1905, he did not mention the République because it would have undermined the drama of his account. And the conviction exuded by his prose was apparently so strong that almost all reference books about the Tour continue to identify 1905 as the year of the first mountain stages.

His representation of the cols in the Pyrenees in 1910 is a masterpiece of rhetoric as well. At that time mass tourism did not yet exist, and for most Frenchmen the Pyrenees were still completely unknown territory, an apparently impassable area between Biarritz, the seaside resort, and Lourdes, the place of pilgrimage, populated by mountain-dwellers with strange customs who spoke an incomprehensible dialect. The public's ignorance gave Desgrange a free hand in writing his previews. He talked about 'bears that came from Spain, looking for food' and cited reports in which the area of the cols was called 'the circle of death'. His conclusion was as follows: 'We have just sent our men into a mysterious, unknown region, and no one knows whether we have not exceeded the limits, whether we are not asking too much from the energy of human beings.' In the days before the Pyreneean stage the tension was constantly raised, and Desgrange naturally did not neglect to advertise his paper obliquely: 'The assault these men will launch on the high slopes of the Pyrenees will be a sublime spectacle for those in a position to observe it, and it provides all of us with an irresistible need to devour, line by line, the narrative of their marvellous exploits.' From the start line in Luchon, *L'Auto*'s reporter wrote: 'Those who have reconnoitred the cols still shudder when they think about them and believe that the riders face an impossible task.' Not so, Desgrange wrote, human perseverance knew no limits, and in his view at least six and possibly even eight riders would manage to conquer the terrors that awaited them.

The Pyreneean stage was 326 kilometres in length, and the roads over the four cols that were part of the course were still unpaved, so that most of the riders had to walk up, holding their bikes by the handlebars. This was in truth an uncommonly difficult assignment even at a time when monster races were unexceptional. Too difficult, according to some of the participants. Victor Breyer, one of Desgrange's employees – Desgrange himself was in Paris – gave an account the next day of a conversation he had with Octave Lapize in 'a stifling heat' on the slopes of the Aubisque:

'Well, what is it, Lapize?'

'What it is, is that you people are criminals. Do you hear me? You can tell Desgrange for me that this kind of exertion should not be demanded from anyone. I've had enough.'

All the same, Lapize kept on going and won the stage, which 46 riders managed to complete in spite of all the sombre predictions. Apparently the task was not really quite as superhuman as all that. But of course Desgrange and his staff did not let on in any way that their previews had perhaps been just a bit exaggerated. According to them, the riders had shown themselves to be 'heroes'. Even the thirteen dropouts qualified for this term, because these had 'come in just a few hours after the closing of the control station'. That their number was so low was due to 'the beautiful, sunny weather'. (A year later, when again there was no evidence of a general slaughter, 'a refreshing shower' was said to have protected the racers from worse.)

In view of the hair-raising scenes for which *L'Auto*'s editors had prepared the public, the Pyreneean stage was, in fact, anti-climactic. Nevertheless it is Desgrange's apocalyptic vision and not the considerably more prosaic reality that has been embedded in the history of cycle sport. As time passed, the weather became ever worse and the organisers were transformed into 'criminals' and 'murderers'. A typical recent version of this myth may be found in a history of the Tour written by the Dutch sports journalist Jean Nelissen in 1973:

> In that year 1910, the most heart-rending scenes were played out in the Pyrenees. In that wilderness of stones and snow, where it was bitterly cold and large hail stones sometimes lashed the arms and legs of the riders, labourers had dug a narrow path between high snowbanks. More than once, exhausted and half-frozen riders were carried shivering into mountain huts. ... A dog-tired rider shouted to Henri Desgranges [sic] that he was a murderer.

Tales like this give an indication of the enormous success of the Tour. Seven years after its laborious beginning it had already grown beyond the status of an ordinary cycle race, and had become a source of myths that were increasingly embellished with the passage of time. The success was in large part the work of Henri Desgrange himself. Without his efforts, this development would certainly not have taken place as quickly and as thoroughly. From the outset he sought, with total conviction, to give his enterprise a legendary dimension. Of course, financial motives played a very important role in this. Desgrange was a businessman above all, and never lost sight of the welfare of his journal, even for a moment. But that is not to say he was a cynic or an actor. He could only have played his role as perfectly as he did because he believed unreservedly in the moral worth of his creation. He grew up in the period after the Franco-Prussian War, when many a Frenchman saw in sports an important means of giving their country the zeal necessary to avenge the defeat. Desgrange was a convinced adherent of this belief, and he was of the view that the Tour could make a key contribution to national recovery:

> Among the thousands who watch the Tour go by, how many are untouched by the blessing of this sport and do not feel ashamed of the physical inactivity of their lives? How many resolve forcefully to begin a new life full of activity and struggle?

According to Desgrange, the riders, specifically the French ones, should set an example to the nation, and he never missed an opportunity to stress their heroism and perseverance, laying it on thick if necessary. He was not prepared to show any understanding for riders who did not conform to his ideal. The story goes that the 1905 winner, Louis Trousselier, cursed him up, down, and sideways during a difficult ascent, whereupon Desgrange is supposed to have answered from the comfort of his sports car: 'Suffering, Trousselier, is the full unfurling of willpower. Prove that you're a man!'

Trousselier apparently answered with a curse. Yet he and his colleagues had every reason to be grateful to Desgrange. Because of the severe exertions the riders had to make during the Tour and the way in which these were glorified in the sports press, cycle racing gained new momentum. The 'giants of the road' conferred enormous prestige on the classics and the other races in which they participated, and when they appeared on the tracks, the velodromes filled up. Their fame reached far beyond the borders of their own country, with the Italian bicycle manufacturers in particular vying for their services. And their incomes rose with their popularity. Maurice Garin earned 12,000 francs for his Tour victory in 1903, factory bonuses included. Four years later Lucien Petit-Breton took in two-and-a-half times that amount. The golden age of cycle sport had begun.

3

The Mighty Marques

In 1903 it had cost Desgrange a lot of effort to interest the industry in his enterprise. Initially the manufacturers were at least as pessimistic about the prospects of the Tour as he was. They doubted strongly whether public interest would be great enough to justify the investments they were being asked to make. They didn't have to engage pacemakers, but the costs of looking after the riders in their service were naturally much higher than for a one-day race. So long did they hesitate that one of the favourites, the German Josef Fischer, a former winner of Paris–Roubaix, Bordeaux–Paris, and many other races, had to advertise for a sponsor in the editorial columns of *L'Auto*.

As public enthusiasm kept mounting during the course of the first Tour, the manufacturers' attitudes changed radically. Desgrange's regulations insisted that riders were to compete strictly as individuals, but the manufacturers very quickly found ways of getting around that. The organisers had been so afraid that too few riders would appear at the start that they permitted dropouts to participate in the remaining stages and do battle for the day's prizes. The manufacturers immediately took advantage of this by engaging riders who had dropped out to serve as disguised pacemakers for their top men, forcing Desgrange in turn to introduce special regulations to prevent it.

By 1904 the manufacturers had completely abandoned their scepticism, but Desgrange did not wish to change the formula that had secured so great a success the year before. His critics had predicted that riders who had to ride without pacemakers would not be willing or able to initiate any attacking moves. They were proved wrong; the progress of the race was extremely lively, with escapes that sometimes went on for hundreds of kilometres. Moreover, several completely unknown riders managed to stay among the ranks of the leaders. Lucien Pothier, 'the terrible butcher from Lens', even finished second, while Jean Dargassies, the Belgian Julien Lootens competing as 'Samson', and several other complete outsiders became involved in the struggle for the top places as well. Their achievements sparked great public enthusiasm and contributed in a major way to the sales of *L'Auto*. As Géo Lefèvre wrote, surprises like this were practically out of the question if these riders, 'alone and without being cared for, had to do battle against the big stars supported by the mighty marques'.

The 'mighty marques' themselves did not care for surprises, and in 1904 they did everything they could to prevent them. In spite of Desgrange's rule that the race must have a strictly individual character, riders such as Dargassies and Pothier were retained by Alcyon and La Française to assist the stars of these companies, among them Hyppolite Aucouturier and Maurice Garin. These were not the only measures taken by the commercial firms. No one doubted that they played an active role in the many irregularities marking the 1904 Tour, just as they had during Bordeaux–Paris a few months earlier, when the first four finishers were disqualified by the French Cycling Federation in the same way that the Tour's first four finishers were.

Desgrange was undoubtedly fully informed about the way in which the big companies tried to get around the regulations, but he made virtually no effort to expose their machinations in his paper. Whatever criticisms he made were aimed exclusively at individual riders. His silence about the role played by the manufacturers in the numerous irregularities was so conspicuous that he was openly accused of having made a deal with the powerful La Française company.

Charges like these were not wholly unfounded. An unmistakable understanding between Desgrange and the big firms did exist. The reason was that, without the cooperation of the most important manufacturers, the Tour simply could not have been organised.

Until the end of the 1920s, *L'Auto* had to finance the organisation of the Tour entirely from its own means. The journal's management was in no position to pay the costs of providing food and accommodation for the participants as well. For some riders this was no problem. During the early years, registration was in principle open to anybody, and enthusiastic amateur cyclists from the well-to-do classes were often unable to resist matching themselves with the 'giants of the road'. One of them was a very rich aristocrat from southern France, Baron Henri Pépin de Gontaud, who took part in the 1907 Tour. Because he did not think himself capable of completing the full distance under his own steam, he secured the services of two professional riders. These were supposed to ride ahead at set intervals so as to order a sumptuous restaurant meal, which could be served the moment the baron himself arrived. One of these two *domestiques* was none other than 'the burly blacksmith from Grisolles', Dargassies, whose career had gone off the rails after a fourth place in the 1904 Tour.

Most of the participants were from decidedly humbler backgrounds, and if they failed to qualify for the daily prizes they sometimes had to try all possible ways of augmenting the per diem of five francs they received from the organisers. For example, in 1907 Marcel Dozol sold picture postcards in the towns where the stages ended, while Jules Deloffre performed somersaults and other acrobatic stunts after completing each stage, and then solicited contributions from the spectators.

The only way of avoiding such a fate was to sign a contract with a bicycle or tyre manufacturer. The riders who had successfully managed this received, aside from a fixed salary, free equipment and extra bonuses when they won a stage. Moreover, their expenses were reimbursed. In exchange for this, the companies exacted not only the right to use their names in advertisements, but absolute loyalty as well. It rarely happened that a rider transgressed against this rule. One of a very few exceptions was Marcel Buysse, who registered for the 1914 Tour of Flanders without his firm's approval. Such an act of independence was so uncommon that the organiser of the race, the journalist Karel van Wijnendaele, was still writing about it in awed tones 30 years later.

To put together a strong field of riders, the organisers of cycle races were totally dependent on the goodwill of the manufacturers, who had all the leading riders under contract and who immediately offered a contract to every new discovery. For this reason alone, Desgrange could not afford to antagonise the major companies. But there was also a second reason: like any other journal, *L'Auto*'s continued existence depended on income from advertising. In that respect the tyre and bicycle manufacturers did not stint themselves. In the event of a victory by one of their riders they almost always placed at least a half-page advertisement. They were all the more willing to do this because *L'Auto* gave them good value for money. The major advertisers could count on being treated highly favourably in the journal's editorials as well as its news columns.

Not only were all kinds of negative publicity totally forbidden, but beyond this the editors rarely passed up an opportunity to give a plug to the products of the most important companies. The Tour de France offered ample opportunity for this. In almost every article, reporters would point to the solid construction of the escorting cars, the dependability of the tyres, and the reliability of the bicycles. A typical example is the comment on Lucien Petit-Breton's Tour victory in 1907, printed opposite a full-page advertisement shared by Peugeot and Dunlop:

> In this way the Argentinian rider [Petit-Breton had spent his childhood in Argentina] has given Peugeot a splendid and incontestable victory, one that goes also to the superb tyres made by Dunlop, a name that appears more and more in connection with the great victories on the road. Petit-Breton quite naturally chose Dunlop tyres. What other brand is better designed to cope with 5,000 kilometres of road? None, and Petit-Breton, taking all due precautions, knew very well what he was doing.

This panegyric aimed at Peugeot and Dunlop did not mean that *L'Auto* had special ties to these two marques. A few years later, when Petit-Breton signed a contract with two other companies and these placed similarly large advertisements, one of the editors promptly wrote: 'We cannot praise too highly the qualities of Automoto and Continental, which have made Petit-Breton an even more extraordinary champion than he already was.'

In spite of the clear relationship between *L'Auto* and the industry, Desgrange realised very well that his interests squared only partly with those of the manufacturers. Nothing stimulated the circulation of his journal like a lively race, full of *coups de théâtre* and unexpected happenings. The factory managers had very different ideas about the ideal progress of a race. Having put a lot of money into a team, they tried to forestall unforeseen events and sought to keep matters under control as much as possible. To achieve these goals they were often willing to come up with large sums of money. The Tour was a potential goldmine for the bicycle manufacturers. Its publicity value was huge, so that when a manufacturer scored a Tour success he could count on an enormous rise in his sales figures. No wonder that the manufacturers were ready to invest tens of thousands of francs in the hope of winning a Tour. The best method to that end was to hire as many likely winners as possible. The big companies fought for the services of the stars, who as a result received monthly salaries of 3,000 francs, excluding bonuses, on the eve of the First World War – a good deal more than a cabinet minister earned in those days.

Initially Peugeot had the edge, winning the Tour in 1906, 1907, and 1908. The next year, though, Alcyon put together a team so strong that the Peugeot people rated their own prospects non-existent, and instead of participating in the Tour organised their own Tour de France for independents (a category of riders who were allowed to take part in races for pros as well as amateurs). The consequence was that Alcyon was scarcely threatened in 1909 and 1910. In 1911 the factory miscalculated, because its well-paid champions were unable to hold their own against a relative outsider, Paul Duboc of La Française. The Tour threatened to turn into a financial disaster for Alcyon, until in the Pyrenees Duboc accepted a water bottle from a spectator. After a few swallows he fell off his bike, seriously ill, and began to vomit up black fluid. Only after several hours had passed was he well enough to continue the race, but of course his chances of winning were gone. Everyone was convinced that Duboc had been poisoned, but Desgrange, who had seen the drama with his own eyes, did not want to hear about such a blemish on his Tour. In L'Auto he dismissed the collapse as a 'minor indisposition'. He did, however, send Calais, Alcyon's race director, home and banned him from ever returning to the Tour.

Thanks to Desgrange's benevolent attitude, Alcyon sustained little harm from the scandal, and the company's sales figures rose so fast that Peugeot could not afford to stay away from the Tour. In 1912 the firm did not invest enough to score a success, but after that year its managers spared neither effort nor expense to retain as many great champions as possible. As a result Peugeot riders occupied the first five places in the final general classification in 1913 and the first three in 1914.

x x x

The big problem for Desgrange was that the rivalry among the companies drove salaries and factory bonuses up so high that only two or three manufacturers, at most, could afford to enter teams that had a chance of gaining the overall victory. When these teams were of roughly equal strength a thrilling battle could result. But it might also happen that one team's supremacy was so great as to preclude surprises. This often prompted manufacturers to withdraw their riders early on so as to avoid spending money unnecessarily. The Alcyon manager sent his riders home after just two stages of the 1907 Tour because, according to him, 'in view of the minimal chance of victory it makes little sense to spend the 40,000 francs the race is costing us'. A day later the manager of Labor followed his colleague's example, so that the riders for Peugeot had virtually no more opposition to worry about in what remained of the Tour. The Alcyon team also quit the struggle long before the end of the Tours of 1908 and 1913, just as La Française did in 1912.

To counter the great influence of the manufacturers' teams, Desgrange kept looking for ways of making sure the Tour rewarded individual performance. In 1908 he thought he had found an effective weapon in the form of 'sealed' bicycles. This system was first used in 1905 when Desgrange created a special category for riders who completed the tour on one and the same bicycle. Whatever damage it sustained had to be repaired without the help of others. The manufacturers showed little initial interest in this category, and the first time it was part of the Tour they entered only unknown riders in it. A few years later they had become conscious of the publicity value emanating from the image of a rider completing 5,000 kilometres on the same bike without the help of others. At the beginning of the century, only one in 40 Frenchmen owned a bicycle; an enormous market lay open, unexploited. The Tour de France constituted a powerful form of advertising for bicycles, not least because it passed through parts of France where bicycle races had never yet been organised. But manufacturers could persuade potential buyers as to the capabilities of their bicycles only when Tour riders used their machines under conditions similar to those encountered by the average Frenchman. And because *he* was not ordinarily accompanied by an escort car carrying spare equipment, it was important for riders to prove that this was not really necessary. The winners of the 'sealed bicycles' category (for control purposes all its parts were provided with lead seals) demonstrated the reliability of their equipment more effectively than those who could exchange their bikes if they broke down. Moreover, it went without saying that *L'Auto*'s editors described the solid dependability of the winning brand in terms of the highest praise.

In 1906, therefore, interest in the sealed-bicycle classification was noticeably greater than the year before. Peugeot entered Lucien Petit-Breton in this category, even though he would otherwise surely have been among the top favourites to win the Tour. 'The Argentinian' gained this dubious honour because he was a better mechanic than Lucien Pothier and Louis Trousselier, his manufacturer's other trump cards, who *were* allowed to change bikes. The management of Alcyon, which had no potential Tour winners signed up that year, went even further and decided to have all its riders compete on sealed bicycles. That year the 'free' category was conspicuously smaller than the 'sealed': eleven to 64. In 1907 the disparity was even more pronounced: eight to 85, and Petit-Breton, again using a sealed bike, succeeded in staying ahead of the riders in the free category, so that he also became the overall winner. This led Desgrange to decree that henceforth all riders must use sealed bicycles. From that moment on, no one was allowed to exchange bicycles or bicycle parts, and if someone had a breakdown, he had to fix the problem himself.

These Draconian measures did indeed lead to *coups de théâtre* but not of the kind Desgrange was very happy with, because they were in conflict with the notion of a pure test of strength, from which sports competitions derive their justification. In almost every Tour some favourite saw his chances for the final triumph go up in smoke due to equipment failure, although *L'Auto* rarely said much about this. When Marcel Buysse, head and shoulders above the competition in 1913, broke his handlebars and wanted to quit in despair, Desgrange's only comment was that under similar circumstances French riders were a lot tougher. He said little more than this about the broken fork Eugène Christophe suffered that same year during the descent from the Col du Tourmalet, as a consequence of which he lost more than four hours. Desgrange, who was riding behind Christophe in his Peugeot convertible ('a marque for which praise is superfluous') wrote only that he waited several minutes and then left the unfortunate rider to his fate 'because the battle up ahead required his attention'. Not until several days had passed did *L'Auto* mention the incident in a brief notice. Six years later, when in the next-to-last stage Christophe again broke his fork and lost two-and-a-half hours, Desgrange could not escape discussing the incident extensively. This time Christophe was in first place with a lead of 28 minutes on his closest rival, and the Tour victory was within his reach. Instead, it went to a Belgian, Firmin Lambot, so that the reverse suffered by 'the old Gaul' was viewed as a national disaster. Desgrange did all he could to build up Christophe's heroic status ('and, like a great warrior overcome by fate, he goes on, looking the god of Destiny who has just defeated him straight in the eye'), and also asked the public to compensate the unfortunate rider for the financial loss he had sustained as a result of his mishap. The appeal yielded 13,000 francs, a splendid result. Less pleasing to Desgrange were the many letters from sports fans who wrote that it was unacceptable for a rider to lose the Tour in this way.

x x x

The 'sealed-bicycle' formula was not only in conflict with the principles of sport, but it also did not effectively counter the influence of the major companies. First of all, manufacturers who commanded the technological expertise necessary to produce bicycles found that copying seals posed no insuperable problem. Nor could Desgrange possibly prevent riders in the same team from shielding each other from the wind or otherwise helping one another. In 1909, therefore, he decided to yield somewhat to pressure from the manufacturers and allow factory teams to compete in the Tour, although he did maintain the system of 'sealed' bicycles. In 1911 he returned to the earlier formula; a year later he once again admitted factory teams. At the same time he emphasised that the introduction of the team system did not mean the race was losing its individualistic character. Desgrange's ambivalence and his never-ending efforts to find a balance between the team system and a race between individuals illustrate perfectly his attitude towards the manufacturers: they were his opponents, but at the same time he depended on them. In the following years, too, he tried through constant rule changes to find a solution to this contradictory stance. But as long as bicycle sales kept growing and the manufacturers' economic power continued, the solution he was groping for was unattainable.

In his long fight against the manufacturers, Desgrange tasted more defeats than victories. Yet without his attempts to limit the influence of the companies, the Tour de France would not have become the monument it is. The effects of Desgrange's behaviour become particularly apparent when the Tour is compared with the cycling event that most resembles it in size and intention, the Giro d'Italia. It was called into being in 1909 by the *Gazzetta dello Sport*, the Italian equivalent of *L'Auto*. The initiative for its founding was rooted in a kind of panic reaction by the editors of the *Gazzetta* to a tip from the bicycle manufacturer Atala to the effect that the *Corriere dello Sport* was considering the launching of a Tour of Italy in collaboration with Atala's chief competitor, Bianchi. This suggests that from the outset the manufacturers in Italy played a much more important role than in France.

Italian sports papers had access to appreciably less money than *L'Auto* or *Le Vélo*. The readers' market in Italy, where more than 40 per cent of the population was illiterate, continued to be so small that before 1919 neither the *Gazzetta* nor the *Corriere* could afford to appear daily. In 1909 the *Gazzetta*'s management were able to finance the organisation of the Giro only with the help of a bank loan and a subsidy from the *Corriere della Sera*, a general-interest newspaper. Of the 65,000 to 70,000 lire in prizes, the organising journal would be paying not even as much as 14,000. The following year the journal accepted the support of the major manufacturers which, just like their French counterparts, regarded a national tour as a key means of publicity in the development of the bicycle industry. Because of this support the manufacturers got far more say in the Giro's organisation than French firms did in the Tour. While Desgrange was in a continuing struggle to keep the Tour a race for individuals, the *Gazzetta* granted the companies a decisive role from the very outset. 'The Giro d'Italia is a team race,' read the opening sentence in the lead article the day the first Giro got underway. This attitude resulted in the Giro's course being much less strenuous than the Tour's, since the major bicycle companies wanted to control the progress of the race as much as possible and, therefore, had very little taste for difficult mountain stages, in which the weather alone could bring about unpredictable outcomes and large numbers of dropouts. Not until the 1930s and 1940s were the Dolomites and the Alps included in the route, by which time the roads through the cols were reasonably manageable. This is one reason why the Giro saw much less of the heroism that in its early years gave the Tour such an important legendary dimension.

The Giro regulations, likewise, took considerably more account of the manufacturers' interests. Indeed, in 1912 only the team classification counted; riders were not ranked individually. This was a manufacturer's dream, which, had it not been swiftly aborted, would soon have threatened the survival of the Giro – Italian cycling fans got a lot less worked up about a duel between Atala and Bianchi than about a battle involving Carlo Galetti, Giovanni Gerbi, and Eberardo Pavesi. A year later the individual formula was restored, but even so the Italian manufacturers got every opportunity to introduce a fairly strict team discipline. That is the chief reason why the use of *domestiques* developed much earlier and more markedly in Italy than in France or elsewhere.

Because the team system suppressed the personal ambitions of most of the participating cyclists, the Giro often witnessed a purer test of strength between the stars than did the Tour. Yet, also as a result of the team system, the Giro lacked one of the most basic elements that has characterised classical tragedy since the ancient Greeks – the struggle of the individual against fate. Even though, at the time they took place, incidents like the reverse suffered by Christophe sometimes proved embarrassing to Desgrange, they, together with 'the heroic battle of man against nature', were among the main ingredients shaping the mythology of the Tour. After his dramatic defeat in 1919, Christophe was at once proclaimed as 'the unluckiest champion who has ever been known'. To reinforce this image, the story of his broken fork in 1913, which had received scant attention at the time, was now resurrected. It was recounted at great length how Christophe had to walk for two-and-a-half hours before he reached the nearest village, Sainte-Marie-de-Campan. There, in the local smithy, he forged a new front fork, which took him another hour-and-a-half. And, as if that weren't enough, he was penalised a further three minutes after the manager of the Alcyon team, Georges Deschamps, who had observed the actions of Christophe (a Peugeot rider) with eagle eyes, complained that he had allowed the blacksmith or his apprentice to operate the drill handle or (sources differ) the bellows.

This tale, embellished with many splendid details by the sports press, was so picturesque that it has completely crowded out the story of Christophe's second broken fork. The French and Belgian sports journals proclaimed Petit-Breton and Marcel Buysse respectively to be the 'moral victor' of the 1913 Tour, but in the 1920s this title was belatedly awarded to Christophe, even though he was fourteen hours behind in the final general classification. And when his admirers wanted to raise a monument to their champion, they located it not in Valenciennes, where he lost the 1919 Tour, but at the smithy in Sainte-Marie-de-Campan. This way they unconsciously testified that the myth was appreciably more powerful than the reality.

x x x

Thanks to the growth of legends of this kind, the Tour became a race which, from the point of view of prestige, towered high above the Giro and all other races. Its aura was so great that outside France only Italy saw the development of an independent cycling scene with its own stars. Even this happened only after the stars of the Tour had given extra cachet to the most important races that came into being at the time – the Tour of Lombardy (1905), Milan–San Remo (1907) and the Giro d'Italia (1909). Belgian cycling still enjoyed so little prestige that riders were taken seriously only after they had scored successes in French races. It took a long time for this to change. Not until after 1907 did the process begin whereby Belgium became the third classic cycling nation alongside France and Italy. The man who gave the impulse to this was Cyriel van Hauwaert, 'the Flemish Lion'. In the spring of 1907 he made his way to the business offices of La Française in Paris in the hope of being taken on for Paris–Roubaix. The management of La Française did not, of course, have the slightest intention of providing a completely unknown rider with well-paid pacemakers, and they fobbed him off with a few spare tyres. But when all the La Française riders had already dropped well back, Van Hauwaert was still in the leading group. He was signed up on the spot and got the use of his team's pacemakers. In spite of a fall, he finished in second place. When he was able to win Bordeaux–Paris two months later, ahead of Tour stars such as Petit-Breton, Trousselier, Christophe, François Faber, Gustave Garrigou, and Henri Comet, he was regarded in Belgium as a national hero. His victories spoke not only to the imagination, though. Van Hauwaert also proved that a successful rider could become rich. In 1908 he went to work for Alcyon, receiving a salary of 3,000 francs per month at a time when a Belgian agricultural labourer got just one franc for a fifteen-hour day. No wonder that many boys in the countryside, as soon as they could afford to buy a bicycle, had but one ambition: to become a racing cyclist. After Van Hauwaert's triumphs the conditions for satisfying this ambition were unusually favourable, for a genuine cycling mania took hold of Belgium. Races were organised all over the place, and even amateurs were able to secure substantial prizes. The year 1908 alone saw the founding of the championship of Flanders and the Tour of Limburg, the revival of the classic Liège–Bastogne–Liège, which had not been raced for fourteen years, and the creation of a Belgian national tour in which well-known Tour de France riders like Petit-Breton, Garrigou and Emile Georget were invited to take part. Five years later Karel van Wijnendaele, editor-in-chief of *Sportwereld*, organised the first Tour of Flanders, a race that came to have almost the same special significance in the 'rich world of Flemish cycling' as the Tour enjoyed in France.

Van Hauwaert's employers naturally wanted him to start in the Tour de France. He dropped out in 1907 and 1908, finished fifth in 1909 and fourth in 1910. After that he no longer appeared at the start. Meanwhile a new generation of Belgian riders had arisen who, inspired by Van Hauwaert's example, also went abroad to find their fortune. For the most part these were the sons of agricultural labourers or small farmers, who had worked hard since childhood and were used to training on the notoriously bad Belgian roads. Therefore they were often better able to cope with the hardships of the Tour and the classic races than were French riders, who mostly came from an urban milieu. Moreover, because their salary demands were fairly modest, the manufacturers were glad to hire their services. Especially after Odile Defraye's victory in 1912, every company wanted some Belgians on its team. Of the 51 men riding for a marque team in 1913 – the remaining participants rode as 'isolated individuals' – 22 were from Belgium, of whom Philippe Thys came in first, Marcel Buysse third, and Firmin Lambot fourth.

Desgrange was little pleased with the new policy of the manufacturers. He celebrated the international character of his race, but he knew that his readers grew genuinely enthusiastic only when a Frenchman was winning the Tour. In 1914, when the superiority of the Brussels cyclist Philippe Thys became so obvious that the circulation of his journal began to fall, Desgrange decided to intervene: in the second-to-last stage he gave Thys a 30-minute penalty on rather dubious grounds, so that his lead on the second-placed Henri Pélissier, a Frenchman, was reduced to less than two minutes. The French public became so excited by the prospect of a compatriot's triumph that they turned out by the tens of thousands to watch the final stage. In doing so they impeded the progress of Pélissier, who had taken a small lead on his rival, with the result that Thys won the Tour after all. Nevertheless Desgrange had achieved his objective: the circulation of L'Auto reached a new record high that day.

The 1914 Tour would be the last for some time. On the day the first stage began, Franz-Ferdinand von Habsburg and his wife were murdered in Sarajevo, and eight days after the Tour's finish in Paris, France declared war on Germany. Desgrange forgot the pious reflections on international fraternisation that had appeared in L'Auto every now and then, and gave thought only to the patriotic function he and many of his countrymen had always assigned to the sport. In red ink he wrote an appeal to his 'dear French boys' to apply the lessons they had learned in the Tour and to slaughter the Prussians, 'those thugs with their filthy square heads', without mercy. Four long years his Tour de France had to make way for le grand Match, as he called the war, a match in which three of the Tour's former winners, Lucien Petit-Breton, Octave Lapize, and François Faber, would find their death.

4

Hard Labour

During the First World War the world of bicycle racing did not grind to a complete halt. A good many races were organised, especially in Italy, which joined the ranks of the belligerents only in 1915. The Tours of Lombardy and Piedmont took place every year as if everything were normal. Milan–San Remo was cancelled in 1915 and 1916 but was back on the programme in 1917. In France, too, several races took place behind the front. The Tour de France and Paris–Roubaix could not be held, of course, but Paris–Tours was run in both 1917 and 1918. Even in German-occupied Belgium races were organised from time to time. The field of riders that participated in these events was seldom very strong. Most of the champions were in military service and were able to appear at the start line, badly trained and badly prepared, only when they were on leave.

Despite the enormous devastation caused by the war, cycle sport revived surprisingly quickly in 1919. The season opened with a seven-stage Circuit of the Battlefields, organised by *Le Petit Journal* in homage to the fallen. The course led through the regions where the fighting had been heaviest, and the roads, disfigured by shell holes and trenches that had not yet been filled in, were very hard to navigate. Belgium's Charles Deruyter came in first, but so many irregularities had taken place that even cycling propagandist Karel van Wijnendaele, who normally took the view that one should not 'wallow in the mud of deceit' if there were also 'beautiful things to be narrated', conceded that one could not say with certainty that the winner had completed the whole distance by bicycle. A few weeks later Paris–Roubaix, too, turned into a murderously heavy slog along roads that, because of hundreds of half-filled shell holes, were even worse than before. Moreover, the weather was abominable, and the landscape through which the riders passed made such a desolate impression with its many craters, ruined houses and charred trees, that a journalist from *L'Auto* christened the region 'the hell of the North', an expression that went down in history.

It was obvious that for the foreseeable future the fat pre-1914 years were no more. The economic position of the French bicycle manufacturers was so bad that even major marques like Peugeot, Alcyon, La Française, Automoto, and Labor could not afford to finance teams of their own. Because they nevertheless wanted to be involved in the sport – if only to deny foreign competitors an opportunity to fill the vacuum – they came together in a consortium that they named 'La Sportive'. This was the only name mentioned in advertisements. Most of the riders engaged by La Sportive raced 'for a jersey and a pair of trousers' and only got their expenses reimbursed. Some stars did get a salary but usually just a small one. Henri Pélissier, second in the 1914 Tour and a former winner of Milan–San Remo and the Tour of Lombardy, had to be content with 300 francs per month, a tenth of what he had received before the war and, given the inflation that had taken place, actually worth much less.

In Italy, which had suffered less from the war, the situation was much more favourable. The major manufacturers did reach agreements to forestall a costly competition among themselves, but they commanded sufficient means to maintain their own teams. Many Belgian and French cyclists (such as the brothers Marcel and Lucien Buysse) who could find no employment in their own countries, went to Italy to enter the service of a manufacturer there, usually for a limited number of races, sometimes for a fixed period of time. There, they were usually given the job of helping one of the current Italian stars, because a compatriot's victory naturally had much greater publicity value for the manufacturers than the success of a foreigner. The *domestique* system reached such an advanced level within Italian teams that the most important races were actually reduced to a tournament between a few top riders. These scored so many victories that they were proclaimed to be super-champions, *campionissimi*. The 1920s were dominated by four men: Costante Girardengo, Gaetano Belloni, Giovanni Brunero, and Alfredo Binda. Between 1919 and 1929 they won every Italian championship, every Giro d'Italia (except for that of 1924 when the large companies kept their riders at home because of a conflict about entry fees), and all but four of the major Italian classics. The big four were not generous with consolation prizes either, such as stage victories in the Giro: of the 113 they won 75. Because of the almost unassailable position of a handful of teams, a style of racing developed that for several decades was held to be typically Italian: in strenuous races the battle was limited to a relatively small part of the total distance; the rest of the time the race was almost at a standstill, with the peloton covering many kilometres in a gentle, easy-going way. To distinguish themselves within this system, Italian riders did not need the degree of toughness and perseverance that were indispensable to a successful Tour cyclist of the 1920s. That is why the *campionissimi* of that time failed utterly in the Tour. All four appeared at the start once (Belloni even twice), but none of them ever made it all the way to Paris. The only Italian who managed to win the Tour in those years, Ottavio Bottecchia, was a very different kind of rider than his more famous colleagues. Precisely for this reason he was unable to beat them in their own country, and he never succeeded in winning an important Italian race.

The difficult state of affairs in which the French manufacturers found themselves after the war prompted Henri Desgrange to make a renewed attempt to turn his old dream into reality: the 1919 Tour would be run as a race for individuals, complete with 'sealed' bicycles. It did not trouble him that a proposal like this could scarcely be realised in 1919: most of the bikes dated from before the war and were in poor condition, while the lamentable state of the roads after four years of war would make heavy demands on them. The result was that only eleven riders succeeded in reaching Paris. Two years passed before Desgrange decided to change his regulation concerning sealed bicycles. When a bike was irreparable in whole or in part, riders were allowed to exchange damaged equipment for new. However, they were obliged to keep the unusable parts so the race judges could inspect them at the finish. This meant, for example, that the Tour winner that year, Léon Scieur, had to ride for 300 kilometres with a buckled wheel on his back. As a result the sprockets dug so deep into his skin that the scars remained visible until his death.

x x x

In 1922 the economy began to improve, so that bicycle sales increased markedly, and the managers of the major companies came to believe the time had come to amend the structure of La Sportive. Of course, they did not care to surrender their extremely favourable position vis-à-vis the riders and so they converted the consortium into a cartel. The manufacturers would each enter their own teams and advertise their own brand names; at the same time they reached agreements about budgets and riders' salaries. Moreover, they decided to maintain a common front against the manufacturers that had not joined La Sportive. They had little to fear from the opposition, because in the meantime they had almost 130 riders, among them all the stars, under contract, a dominance that seemed impossible to overcome.

The main victims of these agreements were, of course, the riders, who were unable to profit from the economic recovery because their salaries and factory bonuses were kept artificially low. At least one man did not take this lying down: Henri Pélissier. In 1921 he had won Paris–Roubaix for the second time and believed this entitled him to a pay-rise. The racing director of La Sportive, 'Marshal' Alphonse Baugé, conscious of his power, would have none of it. Whereupon Henri Pélissier and his brother Francis resigned, and moved to a small independent manufacturer, J. B. Louvet. Pierre Chany writes in one of his standard volumes on the history of French cycle racing that Maisonnas, the managing director of Louvet, originally wanted to engage the brothers just for Paris–Roubaix and promised them a longer-term contract only if one of them were to win the race:

> The stake for the two brothers, who have to triumph over the opposition of 130 riders, is enormous, because the 'Marshal' has given the order: 'These two must not win a single race and above all not Paris–Roubaix! It's up to you to stop them.' Because if a Pélissier does not win, J. B. Louvet's team will withdraw from competition and the two dissidents will be unemployed, forced to go into exile in Italy.

The outcome: Henri Pélissier in first place, Francis Pélissier in second. It sounds like a fairy tale, and that is exactly what it is. The Pélissiers did indeed finish one-two in the 1921 Paris–Roubaix, but they were still employees of La Sportive at that time. Not until the beginning of 1922 did they quit and then sign up with J. B. Louvet. The first major race they competed in for their new company was the Tour of Flanders, in which Henri finished third. He did win Paris–Tours that year, while Francis triumphed in Bordeaux–Paris. That does not, of course, diminish their courageousness in breaking with the consortium, and it is only fair that their rebellion has been expanded into one of the most celebrated legends of cycling. The Pélissiers were extraordinary riders and in many respects assumed a most important place in the cycling world of their time. For example, they developed wholly new insights in the area of training. To get into shape, their colleagues tried to ride as many kilometres per day as they could. The Pélissiers discovered that short, intense exertions are often far more effective. They also experimented with new methods of nutrition. At that time cycling races often lasted for many hours, and most riders were deathly afraid of *la fringale*, the notorious onset of ravenous hunger in which all energy seems suddenly to leave the body. To guard against this, they stuffed themselves before the start with eggs, cutlets, bananas and other kinds of food that lay so heavy on the stomach that they could barely move during the early part of a race. In the morning the Pélissiers limited themselves to a light breakfast, and they preferred to attack in the first kilometres, when their rivals were most vulnerable. They also found out that they had to abstain from alcohol during a race. This was a sensational discovery, because their contemporaries saw only its stimulating effects. Of course all riders knew that the tonic did not last long, but they tried to overcome this by constantly taking new doses. The riders of the Alcyon team drank a whole bottle of cognac during Bordeaux–Paris, augmented by a few glasses of white wine, port, and champagne. Fortunately the riders of that time seldom entered more than forty races annually, for otherwise cirrhosis of the liver would surely have wreaked havoc in the peloton.

Still more important was Henri Pélissier's role as the first rider to take steps to control the power of the organisers and manufacturers. This unquestionably owed much to his background. Most riders came from families which had lived in poverty for so many generations that a life of comfort lay beyond their horizon. They earned more money from cycling than they had ever dreamed of and were not inclined to question their working conditions. Henri Pélissier was from an entirely different background. He was the son of a man who might have been a character in a Balzac novel, a farmer from the Cantal region in the Auvergne who had gone to Paris and built a flourishing milk business there. Henri's father had fiercely resisted his son's plans to become a racing cyclist, an occupation that respectable people in those days ranked little higher than that of a circus clown. Henri had been able to realise his ambition only by running away from home when he was nineteen. In adolescence he had not allowed anyone to tell him what to do, and he had no intention of doing so once he had become an adult. 'He sees every manufacturer as his opponent and every organiser as his enemy,' Desgrange wrote. This merely meant that Pélissier always viewed cycling from the point of view of his own trade, and refused to tolerate manufacturers and organisers placing their own interests above those of the riders. Because this was simply the way things were (as it still is today), Pélissier lived in a permanent state of war with everyone of any significance in cycle sport, starting with Desgrange, who organised almost all important French races in the 1920s and also managed the two biggest velodromes. Pélissier could afford this attitude because he was not only the best but also the most popular rider of his day, and because his stubbornness gained him ever more public support.

What Pélissier objected to most strongly were the long, hard stages of the Tour. The average distance of a stage in the early post-war years was around 360 kilometres, and the longest was fully 482 kilometres. In Pélissier's opinion, in putting together a course like that, Desgrange was confusing 'toughness' with 'brute strength'. As a consequence the Tour was a race for 'workhorses' (by which he meant especially the Belgian riders) and not for 'thoroughbreds' (like himself). In 1919 and 1920 he dropped out after a few stages, and in 1921 and 1922 he did not even appear at the start. His brother Francis faithfully went along with him each time. Eventually Desgrange would recognise that the Pélissiers were right and reduced the average length of stages to 225 kilometres. But that was not until 1927, when Henri's career had all but reached an end.

x x x

In spite of his aversion to the Tour, Henri Pélissier nevertheless did win it in 1923, in his 34th year. Because myths rarely leave room for prosaic elements, the story took shape that he appeared at the start only because he had felt his honour to be under attack by the many taunting articles in which Desgrange claimed that Pélissier was, at his age, no longer physically or psychologically capable of winning a demanding event like the Tour. The truth was much simpler: Henri took part in the Tour because his new employer forced him to. As might have been expected, he had also quarrelled with Maisonnas, the manager of J. B. Louvet. The latter had signed a contract with the Galeries Lafayette in Paris which meant that Francis Pélissier would be followed in Bordeaux–Paris not by a regular team car but by a department store delivery van on which the company's name appeared in large letters. This vehicle was so slow that, when Francis had mechanical trouble, he was forced to wait for many minutes before the van showed up and he lost first place as a result. The Pélissiers had never tolerated this kind of treatment, and they decided to resign. They presented themselves to Automoto, a manufacturer that had recently separated itself from La Sportive, and got a contract on condition that they would participate in the Tour, the company's chief publicity goal. Due also to the support of a very strong team and several shady incidents, such as the poisoning of the 1921 winner, Léon Scieur, Henri Pélissier did indeed become the first Frenchman since 1911 to arrive in Paris wearing the yellow jersey.

For Desgrange, who had seen the circulation of *L'Auto* soar to a new record level of 495,000, everything was thereby forgiven and forgotten. Pélissier's triumph inspired him to scale new lyrical heights and to compare the beauty of his victory to the most brilliant creations of Michelangelo, Corneille, and Richard Wagner. Pélissier was not mollified. He stuck to his criticism of the ridiculously heavy exertions that were asked from riders, and the many rules and regulations that made the race unnecessarily hard for them. For example, in 1920 Desgrange had decreed that a rider had no right to waste anything supplied by his manufacturer and was therefore obliged to arrive at the finish with the same equipment he had left with. That year he looked on in shock as Pélissier, preparing for the sprint to the finish, rid himself of superfluous baggage such as spare tyres, pump, food, and repair materials. Pélissier was not the man to trouble himself about rules like that. Tour stages were so long that the start often took place before dawn, and if it were not yet warm enough he left wearing two jerseys, one over the other. Later he discarded one. During the stage from Le Havre to Cherbourg in the 1924 Tour, he was foolish enough to do this in full view of Eberardo Pavesi, the manager of Legnano, a rival team. The Italian immediately registered a complaint. Pélissier did not deny it, but explained that the jersey he had thrown away was his personal property and he could therefore do with it as he pleased. Desgrange postponed making a decision. However, with a view to possible future sanctions one of the race judges, André Trialoux, could not resist checking before the start of the next stage how many jerseys Pélissier was wearing *this* time. The latter yelled angrily that he was not a school boy and was going to quit the race. He did get underway, but a few dozen kilometres later he and Francis dropped back to the rear of the peloton, after which the brothers withdrew from the race.

Among those following the Tour that year was Albert Londres, known ever since his series of newspaper articles about forced labourers in the Cayenne penal colony as 'the prince of journalists'. Londres was not a sportswriter and knew little about bicycle racing. But like every good reporter he had a nose for what was newsworthy. While all his colleagues stayed with the peloton, he turned around to look for the Pélissiers. He found them in a café opposite the railway station in Coutances, and got an interview that appeared in the next day's issue of *Le Petit Parisien*:

'An impulse?'

'No,' says Henri, 'only we're not dogs.'

'What happened?'

'A matter of no consequence, or rather of jerseys. This morning in Cherbourg a race steward came up to me and without saying a word lifted up my jersey. He wanted to make sure I didn't have two jerseys on. What would you say if I were to lift up your jacket to see if your shirt is really white? I don't care for manners like that. That's the whole story.'

'What does it matter whether you're wearing two jerseys?'

'I can wear fifteen, but I'm not allowed to leave with two and arrive with just one.'

'How come?'

'That's the regulation. Not only are we supposed to ride like beasts, but we're also supposed to freeze or suffocate. That's also part of the sport, it seems ... You've got no idea what the Tour de France is,' Henri says. 'It is a calvary. And the road to Golgotha had only fourteen stations, while ours has fifteen .... And you've seen nothing yet, just wait for the Pyrenees. That is Hard Labour. We have to endure all that. What we wouldn't do to mules, we do to ourselves. We're not idlers, but for God's sake, let them stop pestering us. Torture we put up with, but we don't want to be harassed. My name is Pélissier and not Fido. I've got a newspaper under my jersey. I left with it, I have to arrive with it, otherwise I'll be penalised. If we want to drink we've got to pump the water ourselves. There will be a day when they'll put lead in our pockets because they'll claim that God made humans too light.'

Thanks to this interview the brothers experienced no repercussions from having quit. On the contrary, they became more popular than ever. Their legend was embellished even further by the headline that Londres, mindful of his series about the Cayenne penal colony, placed above his article: 'Forced labourers of the road.'

The Pélissiers did not confine themselves to interviews. A couple of months after the incident in Coutances they took the initial step towards the formation of the first trade union for professional racing cyclists. Just before the First World War such an initiative would have been pointless, because the cyclists were amply compensated for the inconveniences they had to put up with. In 1925 the manufacturers and race organisers were still successful in keeping salaries, bonuses and prizes low, even though more bicycles were being sold than ever before. The Pélissiers therefore found many of their colleagues ready to listen to their plans. In the spring of 1925 the new union swung into action for the first time. The immediate reason was Desgrange's plan to standardise provisions, so that all riders would get lunch bags with the same content, instead of their own favourite food. This system would be first used in Paris–Tours. The union leadership then decided to call a strike.

Desgrange was not about to give in to anybody, least of all to Henri Pélissier. The latter had quite naturally become president of the union, but that did not mean he was the best man for the job. Not only was Pélissier's relationship with the powerful Desgrange extraordinarily bad, but he also had many enemies among the riders, especially among the Belgians. Their French colleagues still regarded them as interlopers, and they frequently had a tough time in the peloton. On such occasions Henri Pélissier often acted as ringleader. The Belgians almost unanimously ignored his strike call, and when a group of French riders caved in to pressure from their employers, who didn't appreciate their riders joining a union and therefore took the same line as Desgrange, Paris–Tours was able to proceed as usual. Simultaneously this spelled the end for the union.

Perhaps Desgrange would have done better to give in to Pélissier, because then the union could have formed a counterweight to the growing power of the manufacturers, who were increasingly undermining the sporting aspects of the Tour. As the economic situation improved, the manufacturers succeeded in creating much the same state of affairs as before the war.

Initially Automoto managed to achieve supremacy. From 1923 through 1926 the top riders for the company, Henri Pélissier, Ottavio Bottecchia, and Lucien Buysse, delivered four Tour victories, two second places, and one third. These successes prompted such an increase in the sales of this marque that its management decided to embark on a major expansion. The moment chosen for this turned out to be inopportune, because in 1926 the number of bicycles sold in France began to stagnate. As a result Automoto's new investments in plant and machinery produced an inadequate return, and the company landed in such financial difficulties that its management decided to forego the Tour and enter only the classics. Although the budget they made available for their racing activities was significantly lower than in previous years, they spent the money so effectively that the company was able to score some resounding victories. The phenomenal Belgian rider Georges Ronsse won several major races, among them Paris–Roubaix in 1927. Initially the Peugeot rider Adelin Benoît was proclaimed the winner and the Belgian national anthem had already been played, but then the arrivals judge suddenly changed his decision. He was none other than André Trialoux, the man whose provocation of Henri Pélissier three years earlier had prompted him and his brother to quit the Tour. When Automoto was forced to close its doors in 1929 and Peugeot took it over, the new management, looking through the records of their former competitor, found a receipt for a substantial amount of money, dated the day of the 1927 running of Paris–Roubaix and signed by André Trialoux...

When Automoto's riders, among them the 1926 winner Lucien Buysse, did not appear in the Tour, the second great marque of those days, Alcyon, had a free hand. In 1927 riders for this company occupied the top four places in the overall classification, and the following year the top five. In 1929, too, an Alcyon rider came in first. The company's dominance was so overwhelming that the race directors of Dilecta and Alleluia decided to resist no longer. They satisfied themselves with the consolation prizes that came their way in exchange for their complaisant attitude. This led to a race so tedious that even *L'Auto*'s baroque descriptions could not make it exciting.

Just as before the First World War, Desgrange tried to change the situation by altering the regulations. His counter-measures were not always apt. To prevent a company like Alcyon from bringing the race almost to a standstill, the way the major manufacturers did in the Giro d'Italia, he turned the flat stages into team time trials. In this way the riders were indeed forced to exert themselves, but the result was that it greatly favoured the strong teams. The best climber in the 1928 Tour, Victor Fontan from the Béarn region, was already hopelessly out of the race by the time the Tour reached the Pyrenees, because he belonged to a weak 'regional' team and had lost more than five hours in the flat stages to the eventual winner, Nicholas Frantz, who benefited from riding in the Alcyon team.

Another problem Desgrange had to cope with was that between 1911 and 1929 the Tour was won by foreigners, with Henri Pélissier's 1923 victory the sole exception. France had few good riders available. The potential champions who should have succeeded Eugène Christophe and Pélissier had for the most part died on the battlefields of Northern France. Only at the end of the 1920s, when a generation that had been too young to be drafted during the war arrived on the scene, would French cyclists once again start booking victories in their national tour. Before that time they were outstripped by cyclists from countries that had sacrificed fewer human lives.

Of course, the frequent foreign victories were not the least bit to the taste of the French public, which had little interest in all those Lambots, Scieurs, Heusghems, Buysses and Dewaeles, none of whom ever had a ringing nickname. The manufacturers didn't really care. Most of them undoubtedly agreed with Ludovic Feuillet, the powerful *director sportif* of Alcyon, who said that he couldn't care less who won the Tour just as long as the winner was riding one of his bicycles. French winners might gain more publicity for a company, but against this stood the fact that they had to be paid more: Automoto paid Henri Pélissier 31,000 francs for his victory in 1923; the Italian Ottavio Bottecchia got a mere 4,000 for *his* victory one year later.

x x x

Desgrange watched unhappily as the major companies shoved one uninteresting winner after another into the limelight, while a promising Frenchman like André Leducq was forced to yield his chances to the Luxembourg rider Nicholas Frantz, of whom nothing more striking could be said than that he was 'caution personified'. After Frantz's victories in 1927 and 1928, Desgrange played with the idea of replacing the manufacturers' teams with national teams. Because he feared the opposition of the manufacturers, he opted for another solution: once again he reached back to the individual formula. It was, of course, totally unrealistic to imagine the power of the major companies could be broken in this way, and Desgrange had to look on helplessly as the new regulation was ignored in every possible way. The irregularities reached their peak when the wearer of the yellow jersey, the Alcyon rider Maurice Dewaele, became ill in Grenoble and was physically dragged across the Alps by the other members of his team. They were able to do this with impunity because Desgrange could not afford a fight with his biggest advertiser and, furthermore, had to preserve the illusion that the Tour was being raced fairly. At the end, Desgrange decided to do no more than punish the man who had finished second overall, Joseph Demuysère, also riding for Alcyon, and to leave the rest of the results untouched.

This time Desgrange's mind was made up: the formula for his race had to be radically changed. The circulation of *L'Auto*, which had remained steady since 1923, began to drop quite markedly for the first time since the war. It was clear the future of the Tour was at risk. On 25 September 1929, he announced that in 1930 his Tour would be contested by national teams. Even before the manufacturers had been able to come up with a considered response, Wall Street experienced the stock market crash that rang up the curtain on the greatest economic crisis of the twentieth century. One of the consequences was that the power of the bicycle manufacturers came to an end, thereby opening a wholly new era in cycle sport.

5

Lessons in Obstinacy

With his plan of having national teams contest the Tour de France from 1930 onwards, Desgrange hoped to bring an end to the manufacturers' machinations that had made recent Tours boring. To restrict the influence of the major companies as much as possible, he even decided to have riders compete on bicycles of an 'unknown make' that would be made available by the race organisation. Participants in the Tour had to check in 48 hours before the start with their own saddles and handlebars; these were then mounted on yellow-painted frames that carried only the name of the organising journal. It went without saying that the Tour organisers would also pay the costs of meals and rooms for the cyclists.

Of course Desgrange could not take these radical steps without the cooperation of the manufacturers. After all, they had the power to forbid their riders to participate in the Tour. But Desgrange had the worsening economy on his side. Most of the smaller companies were actually more than pleased that, given the difficult economic situation in which they found themselves, they did not have to pay for the food, accommodation and equipment of their riders. The only *directeur sportif* who protested loudly against the new plans was Alcyon's Ludovic Feuillet, but Desgrange was more or less able to reconcile him to the new formula by leaking the information that the 'unknown make' the riders would use was Alcyon. Thereupon Feuillet decided not to carry out his threat to keep his riders from appearing in the Tour. But he did find it necessary, as a kind of protest, to withhold several strong men, such as the Belgians Gaston Rebry and Julien Vervaecke (who would otherwise certainly have been selected for the Tour) for another, much less important race.

Desgrange remained dependent on the big companies for a second reason. It was their custom to place large advertisements in *L'Auto* when one of their riders won a stage, and the income this yielded was essential to the journal's continued existence. Desgrange therefore permitted the manufacturers to give publicity to the entire year's achievements of the cyclists in their service, even though they used different equipment during the Tour. This was an arrangement from which both sides were able to profit, but through which the companies indirectly recovered some of their influence on the course of the race. In 1931 Antonin Magne would almost lose the victory because of it. The Depression had led his employer, Alleluia, to withdraw from racing that year and, in spite of his third place in the 1930 Tour, Magne had failed to find a new sponsor. His equipment came from a small constructor in the Cantal region where he was born. Because this outfit produced for the local market only, its owner had no intention of placing large advertisements in the organising journal, which in any case were too costly for him. To his dismay Desgrange saw an important source of income escaping from him and tried discreetly to persuade Magne's team-mates to lend their leader less generous support. Because none of the riders of the French team was capable of assuming Magne's role, and none wished to forego his share in the prize for the overall victory, Desgrange's efforts failed. The Tour director did not mean to make the same mistake twice. When André Leducq, winner in 1930 and 1932, broke his contract with mighty Alcyon in 1934 and entered the service of a small new marque, Mercier, which to make things worse was managed by Francis Pélissier, he simply did not get permission to start the Tour.

Desgrange's decision to assume responsibility for the costs of equipment and the physical welfare of the riders obviously meant a heavy burden for the organising journal. It could carry this burden only because Desgrange had succeeded in tapping new sources of income. These came mainly from business sectors that were not involved directly in the manufacture of bicycles or bicycle components, but still wanted to make use of cycle racing to advertise their products. Galeries Lafayette's attempts to do so in 1922 had not been particularly happy, but since then it had become ever more common in important races for the peloton to be followed by one or more vehicles carrying advertising. This had little impact, though, because the spectators had usually dispersed well before the cars came by. This changed only in 1930, when the Menier chocolate company gained permission from Desgrange to have a company car precede the riders. The management of the company seized this opportunity to launch an enormous publicity campaign. They staffed a company lorry with employees who distributed fully half a million caps with logos, as well as several thousand kilos of chocolate bars to the waiting public. At the tops of the cols the Menier crew poured hot chocolate for the riders and their followers, while the company also awarded a sort of mountain prize.

The campaign became so successful that many enterprises followed Menier's example and also sent an advertising vehicle to accompany the Tour. Some of them, such as Perrier, Pernod, Martini, and Banania, would be present in the sport for years. All these businesses received the same preferential treatment in *L'Auto*'s pages as the regular advertisers. The journal went so far as to publish a special supplement, with an overview of the bonuses that the members of the advertising caravan were making available, in which the editors naturally did not neglect to praise the products of their sponsors. In Desgrange's eyes this was undoubtedly but a small sacrifice to make for their cooperation. Of course, he effectively took on the obligation to attract these firms, but this bothered him less than his dependence on the bicycle manufacturers, who tried constantly to interfere with the race. The *'extra-sportif'* firms also exercised a certain influence on it, although only indirectly at the beginning, for example by offering bonuses. And yet Desgrange's initiative had more far-reaching consequences than he probably suspected. Until this time professional cycle racing formed a more-or-less closed world that was in principle completely in the hands of people who depended directly on it, such as cyclists, organisers, sportswriters, and representatives of the bicycle industry. By making himself partly dependent on the advertising caravan, Desgrange opened the door to outsiders for the first time, although so far only by a crack.

Another problem Desgrange had to solve when he introduced his national-team formula was how to assemble a strong international field of cyclists. There were five countries capable of putting together a more-or-less fully-fledged national team: France, Belgium, Italy, Germany, and Spain. In the Netherlands road races were still officially banned and in Great Britain they were simply not part of the racing culture, which was dominated there by track-sprinting. Countries like Luxembourg and Switzerland had only a few first-class riders, while those from outside Europe, such as the Australian Hubert Opperman and the Japanese Kisso Kawamuro, remained isolated individuals.

It took little effort to persuade the Belgian Cycling Federation to designate a team. Because Belgium did not possess a bicycle industry of any significance, all the strong Belgian cyclists rode for French companies, and for that reason alone they could not afford to stay away from the Tour. The only problem was the 1929 winner, Maurice Dewaele. Desgrange had announced that he himself would make the final selection of the teams, and since he was convinced Dewaele had not won the 1929 Tour fairly and squarely, he did not want to see him enter the 1930 race. The Belgian federation, and Karel van Wijnendaele as its representative, tried to change Desgrange's mind, and accepted his stipulation only after he had promised that Dewaele's ban would be lifted in 1931.

The participation of the Italians proved more problematic. It was by no means a sure thing that they would show up at the start. In 1930 cycle sport did not yet have much of an international character. Not until 1927 had a world championship been established, and it was the sole race in which the strongest riders from each country appeared. The other races were contested mainly by riders from the countries where they were held, with the exception of the major road races in France in which Belgians riding for French companies were never absent. Most Italian cyclists made only infrequent appearances outside their national boundaries. The manufacturers in whose service they worked aimed their products almost exclusively at the domestic market, and they were rarely willing to finance a team in a race outside Italy.

Desgrange tried to break through this attitude because he quite rightly believed that without strong Italian representation his Tour would not be credible as a race between national squads. He had his eye on one man in particular: Alfredo Binda. Now that Costante Girardengo and Gaetano Belloni were in their late thirties and Giovanni Brunero had ended his career, Binda had scarcely any serious competition left in Italy. In 1927 he had succeeded in winning every race in which he competed, with the exception of Milan–San Remo (where he was second). He had also won the world championship and the Giro d'Italia, in twelve of whose fifteen stages he triumphed as well. Binda was a gifted climber, a formidable *rouleur*, and an outstanding sprinter. Furthermore, his style was so smooth that his colleagues claimed he could ride for 200 kilometres with a cup of milk on his shoulders and not spill a drop. He was so superlatively good a rider that he never succeeded in becoming very popular among his compatriots, not even on chauvinistic grounds, because he rode almost exclusively against other Italians. In spite of this, Binda's prestige was enormous, and Desgrange needed his presence in the Tour so badly that against all his principles he secretly offered the *campionissimo* a huge appearance fee. Financially it was a good year for Binda, because he had also received a fabulous amount of money from the organisers of the Giro so that he would *not* take part. His dominance in the last three Giros had been so overwhelming that there was not an ounce of suspense to the race, and the circulation of the organising *Gazzetta dello Sport* had sunk to a disappointing level.

The financial conditions offered to him for his participation in the Tour were so favourable that Binda allowed himself to be persuaded, although after long hesitation. And Desgrange got value for money. Merely because of the announcement that the *campionissimo* would appear at the start, *L'Auto*'s circulation shot up, and when Binda was amiable enough to allow the new French idol, Charles Pélissier, younger brother of Henri and Francis, to beat him in the first-stage sprint, sales of the journal, which had never been above half a million, rose to more than 600,000.

From that moment on interest in the Tour mounted from day to day. Binda dropped out halfway through the Tour, but the French team went from strength to strength. They won twelve of the 21 stages and in the final overall classification occupied first, third, fifth, sixth, and ninth place. For the first time the Tour became a truly *national* happening in France. The general-interest newspapers carried more Tour news than ever before. That year, too, radio made its Tour debut and devoted three broadcasts per day to the Tour: a general impression at noon, coverage of the finish in the afternoon, and a postmortem at night. The newsreels that preceded the main feature in cinemas also paid regular attention to the Tour.

x x x

The members of the French *équipe nationale* owed their new-found popularity not just to their victories. The national-team formula gave a new meaning to their whole way of riding. Desgrange stipulated in the regulations that a certain degree of team spirit would be tolerated, provided it were not abused. By this he was referring to the kind of incident that had taken place in 1929, when members of the Alcyon team had hauled the indisposed Maurice Dewaele over the Alps. Desgrange, who had not yet altogether abandoned the idea of an individual race, abhorred such behaviour. For the riders, on the other hand, it was the most natural thing in the world, and when the wearer of the yellow jersey, André Leducq, took a serious fall in the Alps and fell twelve minutes behind his nearest rival, his team-mates reacted in precisely the same fashion as the Alcyon riders the year before. With the injured Leducq in train, the full team went in furious pursuit of the leaders, whom they caught just before the finish. Then they manoeuvered their top rider into such a favourable position that he won the stage. This episode still ranks as one of the high points in Tour history, and the riders who managed to put this masterpiece together were immediately hailed as heroes.

It stood to reason that the members of the Alcyon team could not expect the same response. As far as the public was concerned they were mere hirelings serving the interests of a commercial enterprise. Now that cyclists were riding for *la patrie*, similar sacrifices could be presented as expressions of 'friendship' or 'patriotism'. Due also to the dramatic radio report that Jean Antoine and Alex Virot made of the pursuit, and to a photograph of a bleeding, weeping Leducq that would later inspire the sculptor Anton Breker in creating his 'Wounded Warrior', the event made such a deep impression that it gave rise to a swelling of general national pride and even made it to the front page of the political dailies such as *L'Avenir*, in whose pages Maurice Duval wrote:

> Do you take an interest in accounts of the stages in the Tour de France? You should. These courageous young men daily give us extraordinary lessons in endurance, energy and perseverance. Yesterday's lesson was the most beautiful of all, because our young men had the opportunity to add to this bouquet of rare qualities these two exquisite flowers: the most affecting camaraderie and the most splendid sense of honour!

The press invariably depicted the French riders as a 'team of friends', and that was also how they presented themselves to the public. In numerous photos they appear riding side by side, arms over each other's shoulders. André Leducq later revealed that he never really could stand Charles Pélissier, with whom he had been constantly coupled in track races, and that he had cooperated with him for business reasons only. A key reason for Leducq's dislike of

Pélissier was financial in origin. Leducq arrived in Paris in 1930 wearing the yellow jersey, but Charles Pélissier was the real winner of the Tour. After the Tour the appearance fee that Leducq received for track races and criteriums rarely amounted to more than 2,500 francs, whereas his team-mate got at least 3,000 and more commonly 3,500 or 4,000 francs per appearance. Leducq protested to the track managers, but in vain. What mattered to the public was not how the riders performed in races but how they were depicted in the media. And in this respect Charles Pélissier easily trumped Leducq. In 1929, when, other than one stage victory in the Tour he had done scarcely anything of note, L'Auto proclaimed him to be the most popular cyclist in France. Of course he owed this in large part to the legends that had been spun around his brothers Henri and Francis. At the start of his career, in fact, Charles behaved completely in accordance with the public image of the Pélissiers. The first time that his name cropped up in the columns of L'Auto was during the Tour of 1925, when he came to the Tourmalet as a spectator in order to shout to the passing cyclists that they were crazy to exert themselves in this way and would do better to go home. This was wholly in the spirit of Henri and Francis. The difference was that they had done enough to have earned the right to speak. That was not true of Charles, who had turned professional two years earlier, but was still waiting for his first victory. The next day Henry Decoin wrote in L'Auto:

I know Charles Pélissier only because of his brothers Henri and Francis, who have accomplished admirable things. And I know that Charles Pélissier is a bicycle rider only because he walks around dressed up as one. But however much I search through the sports pages, I can't find a Pélissier with the Christian name Charles. Henri and Francis are peacocks. They have beautiful feathers, and now and then Charles filches a couple and glues them on his back and parades like a jay along the boulevards of sport.

In other words, Charles's relations with the press did not start very promisingly, and he quickly decided to change his attitude. In contrast with his brothers, he never had to fight for anything, and the role of rebel was foreign to him. Moreover, his athletic endowments were not great enough to enable him to take on the established order singlehandedly. He *did* possess other qualities. His highest trump card was his appearance, to which he paid so much attention that he acquired the nickname 'Beau Brummel'. He looked like a matinée idol and during every Tour he received dozens of marriage offers, which he allowed his wife, 'la Pélissette', to answer. In their time his brothers had introduced new training methods and standards of nutrition, and Charles, too, made a contribution to the development of cycle racing. He was the first cyclist to wear white socks because they contrasted so beautifully with his tanned legs.

On the insistence of his wife, Charles sought to get closer to Henri Desgrange. Although the latter had some misgivings at first, he gradually became more favourably disposed to the youngest Pélissier. During the 1930 Tour no rider was mentioned as often in *L'Auto* as Charles Pélissier. In past years Desgrange had always disapproved of mass sprints, but now that 'Beau Brummel' took part in them and often won them to boot, Desgrange gave them the same impassioned consideration as the ascent of the Galibier and Tourmalet.

x x x

The media have never had so much power in the world of cycle sport on the road that they can make a star out of nothing, and if Charles Pélissier had not been able to win a goodly number of stages in the Tour he would have remained an obscure minor cyclist. But probably no other rider has gained so much fame on the strength of so little achievement. He himself was well aware that he could never reach the top as a rider, and he therefore expended his energy chiefly on the cultivation of his personal image, an art he mastered far better than his colleagues. His finest hour came in 1931, when his team's top rider and the eventual winner of the Tour, Antonin Magne, fell back in the Alps because of a sudden and severe collapse – that unexpected complete loss of strength the French call a *défaillance*. Under the eyes of the assembled press Pélissier performed a masterpiece. He pulled ahead of Magne, and with the latter at his wheel he made up almost four minutes in 60 kilometres. He did not permit any of his team-mates to take the lead at any time. He exhausted his physical resources so completely that he collapsed after reaching the finish. Desgrange, who had already referred to

Charles Pélissier as the Voltaire and the Euripides of cycling, could think of only one superlative that would do justice to Pélissier's suffering: he compared him to Christ on Golgotha and concluded his article with one of those lyrical outpourings to which Charles Pélissier inspired him more than once:

> Where art thou, Pindar, to sing the praises of our Charles in your Epinicia? Why wert thou not with us, Corneille, prince of tragedy? Thou shouldst have been able to discern new feelings in the human soul. Because everything was there: poetry, majesty, grief, and sport as well.

Charles Pélissier became the first racing cyclist to gain entry into the *beau monde*. He associated with aristocrats, politicians, writers, and painters, and was intimately acquainted with the singers Mistinguett and Maurice Chevalier. He even twice played the lead role in a film. After his 30th birthday he mostly allowed himself to be admired at cycling tracks, where benevolent organisers helped him to win victories he could no longer secure by his own efforts. And long after his cycling career had come to an end, he continued to be successful in using his name to make lots of money.

So expansive and surprising was the Tour's popularity that came about through the successes of Charles Pélissier and his team-mates that Desgrange was ready to abandon all his earlier principles for it. In the 1920s he had kept making rules that were meant to prevent mass sprints; in 1932 he sought to encourage them by giving the first three finishers in each stage bonuses of four minutes, three minutes, and one minute. In this way he hoped to help secure a Tour victory for Charles Pélissier, who would have gained 56 minutes in 1930 had this rule been in effect. In vain: a few weeks before the Tour began, Charles broke his collarbone and could not appear at the start. Instead it was André Leducq, like Pélissier an outstanding sprinter and a mediocre climber, who profited from the new rule. He won a total of 30 bonus minutes, 24 more than the German Kurt Stöpel, whom he led in the final general classification by 24 minutes and three seconds.

Another principle Desgrange abandoned was the old ideal of a race between individuals, which he had nourished ever since the first Tour. The public had been wildly enthusiastic about the manner in which the French cyclists had assisted each other, and had even drawn from this the moral lessons that were so dear to Desgrange. So now he took steps to strengthen team cooperation. In 1934, for example, he finally permitted team-mates to give each other components in the event of a breakage, a regulation that had been in effect in the Giro d'Italia for years.

This rule change introduced an element into the Tour that would become a source for new legends: the self-sacrifice. It produced a hero in the very first year, the rookie René Vietto. He came from Cannes and was already, at age eighteen, unbeatable in the Côte d'Azur mountain courses. In his first Tour he won three of five Alpine stages, thereby securing a huge lead in the mountain classification. He couldn't do much more than climb, though, with the consequence that at the foot of the Pyrenees he trailed the wearer of the yellow jersey, his team-mate Antonin Magne, by a good 35 minutes.

The drama began in the first Pyreneean stage, when Magne fell during the descent from the last col and broke his front wheel. Vietto offered him his own front wheel, but because it did not fit Magne instead accepted that of Georges Speicher, who had also stopped. Speicher, who was reigning world champion and winner of the 1933 Tour, naturally ranked higher in the team hierarchy than Vietto. Besides, he was held to be the best descender of his day and because the remaining kilometres were down hill, he would be able to render very valuable services to Magne. Speicher accepted Vietto's front wheel, succeeded in installing it on his own bike, and in the company of Magne set out in pursuit of the leading group. Vietto had to wait for the team car to show up and lost four minutes. The next day Magne had yet another breakdown: he broke his chain. Vietto gave him his bicycle and in this way lost another four minutes.

Incidents of this kind happened so often during a Tour that Henri Desgrange barely mentioned it in the next day's issue of L'Auto. But while Vietto was waiting for the equipment car during that first Pyreneean stage, someone took a photo of him that would change his life. The picture showed a sobbing Vietto sitting on a low wall with his bike, minus its front wheel, leaning next to him. It is one of the most famous documents in the iconography of the Tour. In most prints the spectators on the right side have been carefully cropped out of the picture so as to strengthen the image of abandonment. One of these spectators, recognisable by his pith helmet and Bermuda shorts, was the later Tour director Jacques Goddet, who at that time was writing a daily column in *L'Auto* under the pseudonym 'l'Ami Bini'. The scene inspired Goddet to write a touching article about the young Vietto, who had felt himself morally compelled to sacrifice his own chances for those of the veteran Magne. That Vietto had relinquished his wheel to Speicher and not to Magne was a detail that would have upset the sublime simplicity of the tale too much and therefore went unmentioned.

The article struck a chord, to the point that almost every newspaper in France copied it in one form or another. To make the story even more dramatic, most journalists added to it the claim that without his sacrifice Vietto would probably, not to say certainly, have won the Tour. This version was so appealing that it found general acceptance. The result was that during the homage to the cyclists at the end of the Tour Vietto got a much bigger ovation than the winner, Magne. The latter was not permitted to ride his victory lap by himself; the spectators did not rest until Vietto had joined him. Banners were unfurled with the words: 'Long live Vietto, the moral winner of the Tour.' As Henri Desgrange wrote in his postmortem, this was nonsense. Vietto's services to his team's top rider had cost him less than nine minutes, while his arrears in the final classification amounted to very nearly a full hour. But Desgrange's words did not make the slightest impression. 'A legend is born and no one will dare to attack it. It is too affecting,' the journalist Georges Briquet wrote. And he was right. In 1934 Vietto earned so much in appearance fees for criteriums and track races that he needed to appoint a manager to look after his finances. He chose André Trialoux, the crooked arrivals judge of Paris–Roubaix in 1927. What happened next was predictable: within a couple of years, Vietto had lost all his money. Although he never again won an important race, he did manage to restore his fortunes. Until the end of his career fifteen years later, Vietto, who gained the nickname 'King René', was able to live off his legend. Every defeat he suffered in the Tour – and there were many of them – became a new victory because it made his 'sacrifice' in 1934 still more poignant, still more heart-rending.

Practically everyone in the cycling world thought he was a pain, from the mechanics and masseurs who were mostly blamed for his defeats, to fellow-riders who were irritated by star-like pretensions that were not justified by achievement. But he remained so popular with the public that all attempts to reduce his myth to normal proportions were doomed to failure. The journalist Gaston Bénac discovered that Vietto had not, as he always insisted, worked in the Hotel Majestic in Cannes before becoming a professional cyclist but in a prosaic telegraph office. Bénac's revelations had no effect at all; even serious reference books continue to relate Vietto's own version of the truth.

In 1934 Vietto became the symbol of the sacrificial spirit within the French national team, but he was unable to keep this role for even a year. Since he knew very well that he had lost the Tour because of his weak performance during the early stages, and not because of his 'sacrifices', he concentrated his training in the spring of 1935 on riding flat roads, using particularly big gears. He even went to live in Northern France for a while in order to get experience on the cobblestones. As a result he really did become a better *rouleur* but lost some of his capacity as a climber. It was therefore Georges Speicher, the 1933 winner, who was the leading Frenchman after the Alps, and not Vietto. Unfortunately Speicher became ill between the Alps and Pyrenees, and because he did not feel he could cope with a very high tempo, at the start of the long initial Pyreneean stage from Perpignan to Luchon (325 km) he instructed his team-mates to slow down the race as much as possible. Vietto simply ignored this, and after 75 kilometres he went on the attack. The worst part was that he proved incapable of sustaining it. He was caught by the Belgians Sylvère Maes and Félicien Vervaecke and finished twenty minutes behind them. Speicher was still further back and lost any chance of final victory.

Speicher accused Vietto of betrayal, of course, but the latter defended himself by pointing out that even before his action relations within the team had been far from good. After all, nothing much was left to hold the French squad together. In the 1930 Tour the riders had agreed to share the prizes, and thanks to their superb team spirit they had earned a large sum of money. This was particularly welcome because the Depression had forced the manufacturers to make major savings on salaries. But very different sources of income soon appeared. Thanks to the French successes and the way the press wrote about them, lots of people wanted to see the heroes of the *équipe nationale* with their own eyes. All over France criteriums and track races were organised in which the riders who had distinguished themselves in the Tour needed to do little more than make an appearance. The appearance fees they received were usually multiples of the modest wages they received from their employers. Charles Pélissier, the best-paid cyclist in France, received a salary of 33,000 francs in 1930. His share of the Tour purse was roughly of the same magnitude. His contracts for track races and criteriums earned him more than 200,000 francs. Although only the big stars received that kind of money, even riders of lesser stature could earn a tidy amount in the form of appearance fees. The number of criteriums kept increasing in the 1930s, and the organisers and sponsors paid large sums to attract as strong a field as possible. With this in mind, few French riders could resist the temptation to play as conspicuous a role in the Tour as they could manage. A self-effacing rider might be of great value to his team, but knew that his chances of getting criterium contracts were slight.

It was not surprising, then, that by 1935 little remained of the French national squad's vaunted team spirit. The inevitable result was that their successes diminished in number. Roger Lapébie was able to win the Tour in 1937, but so many irregularities had to take place to make that possible that the entire Belgian team, the wearer of the yellow jersey included, withdrew a few days before the end, and the winner, just like Dewaele in 1930, was prevented by Desgrange from taking part in the next year's race.

The golden age of the *équipe nationale* ended in 1938, when Antonin Magne and André Leducq, each riding in his last Tour, crossed the finish in Paris as joint first in the stage, their arms around each other's shoulders. The public came to their feet and exploded in loud cheering, not only for the two old champions but also for this last flash of the 'comradeship' that had made the French national team and the Tour more popular than ever.

Outside France interest in the Tour also grew noticeably. The national formula squared perfectly with the chauvinistic feelings which even today are still among the most important wellsprings of the enthusiasm of sports fans. In consequence, the fame of the Tour grew to the point that even Italian riders found it increasingly difficult to stay at home. Alfredo Binda, who had reluctantly appeared at the start in 1930, quit the contest after a victory in the major Pyreneean stage because he thought he had done enough to justify his high appearance fee. Thereby he cleared the way for Learco Guerra, 'the Mantua Locomotive', whose three stage victories and second place overall gained him a degree of popularity in Italy that he would not have been able to capture through domestic races alone.

The Tour became so important that ever more Italian cyclists with established reputations tried their luck in France. From 1919 to 1929 it happened only four times that a rider who had a victory in the Giro to his credit started in the Tour de France. From 1930 to 1938 this occurred thirteen times.

Benito Mussolini's government began to interest themselves in the Tour as well by 1937 for its propaganda value. During the 1936 Berlin Olympic Games the Fascist authorities had seen how important sport could be for the image of a totalitarian regime, and were therefore most eager for a victory in the greatest bicycle race in the world. The rider who was supposed to take care of this was the man who had won the 1937 Giro d'Italia convincingly. Because its course, which included the Dolomites for the first time, resembled the Tour far more closely than earlier editions, people were confident that he had a better chance of success than the other Italian stars of the 1930s. His name was Gino Bartali.

Bartali was discovered in 1935 when he was riding in Milan–San Remo as an 'independent' without a contract, and took a seemingly commanding lead on the two big stars, Learco Guerra and Giuseppe Olmo, even though he was stuck in a low gear because mud had got into his derailleur. The prospect of his victory greatly worried the editor-in-chief of the sponsoring newspaper, the *Gazzetta dello Sport*, Emilio Colombo, who did not like unknowns to win, especially if they were, as in this case, wearing a jersey without a company name. Colombo was known as the Italian Desgrange and was at least as crafty as his French counterpart. In his car he took up a position alongside the leading rider and, showing great interest, began to question him. Bartali was so thrilled to be interviewed by a celebrity like Colombo that he did not notice that the latter gradually reduced speed. When Guerra and Olmo, aided by the support vehicles, had established contact, the question-and-answer session came to an end. In the sprint Bartali, still stuck in a low gear, did not have a chance.

In spite of this unsuccessful start, Bartali became a star in his first year. He won the Italian championship, several Spanish races and the mountain classification in the Giro, in which he emerged as a wonderful climber. In 1936 and 1937 he won the Giro d'Italia, and in 1937 he also seemed set to win the Tour when, during a descent, he ended up crashing into a mountain stream. He managed to retain the yellow jersey but caught a chill from the ice-cold water and had to drop out a couple of days later.

The next year he was under orders to attune his entire season to winning the Tour. The authorities would not even give him permission to take part in the Giro, because they were afraid he would exert himself too much and become fatigued. This time they succeeded in their objective. On the Col d'Izoard Bartali won the stage, and with it the Tour, with such crushing dominance that Desgrange promptly hailed him as the best bicycle racer of all time.

In the past Desgrange had usually reserved pronouncements of that kind for French cyclists, but this time he was certainly not displeased about an Italian *campionissimo*'s victory. It fitted very nicely into the changes the Tour was undergoing at a time when it was becoming ever harder to finance the organisation of the Tour from the sales of *L'Auto*. In 1933 the journal's circulation had reached a record of 364,000 per day on average (with a peak of 730,000 in July), but since then sales had steadily declined. In 1938, the last full year before the war, average daily circulation dropped to just over 200,000. This did not mean that interest in the Tour was dropping; far from it. It was precisely the Tour's success that created problems for *L'Auto*. Because of the public's growing enthusiasm, the general-interest dailies started to pay so much attention to the Tour that it was increasingly unnecessary to buy a sports paper. *L'Auto* sustained its biggest blow from *Paris-Soir*, which, thanks to a staff of 40 led by Gaston Bénac and equipped with two airplanes, five cars, five motorcycles and a bus, was able from 1935 onwards to publish an extra edition every evening with an account of the day's stage which had just finished, whereas readers of *L'Auto* had to wait until the next morning to read about it.

Desgrange realised he could do nothing about this state of affairs. The days when his journal could monopolise information about the Tour were gone forever. He was even willing to lend all possible assistance to the journalists who came to his Tour from all parts of Europe. Some of them actually got official positions as team directors, such as Karel van Wijnendaele and Joris van den Bergh, who took charge of the Belgian and Dutch riders respectively. After all, the new developments had advantages as well. Now that the Tour made international news – and victories by foreign celebrities such as Gino Bartali contributed to this – French communities attached ever more value to serving as the start or finish to stages, or to giving right of passage to the caravan, and they were prepared to pay for it. Moreover, it became easier to attract sponsors.

Especially after the Popular Front government led by Léon Blum gave workers the right to paid vacations, the number of people who saw the Tour go by grew enormously. In the past the riders had cycled along deserted roads in the mountains; during ascents they now often had to make their way between thick hedges of spectators. All these spectators may not have gathered much about the progress of the race, but they did have an excellent view of the advertising caravan that preceded the cyclists. Businesses were therefore willing to pay ever more money to secure a place in it. As a commercial enterprise, then, the Tour was in a phase of fundamental change when the Second World War broke out in 1939.

6

Sweat of the Gods

Just as after the First World War, cycle racing recovered fairly quickly after 1945. The Tour de France could not yet be held in 1946, but aside from this a full racing programme was in place. In Belgium two big races for professional cyclists were actually added, Ghent-Wevelgem and the Omloop Het Volk. All the same, there was an important difference between the situations in 1919 and 1946. After the First World War, cycle racing continued to be dominated for years by men who had already made reputations for themselves before 1914, whereas most of the major races in 1946 and afterwards were won by riders who had been quite unknown in 1939. The first classic of the season, Milan–San Remo, turned into a crushing victory for a new talent, Fausto Coppi who, after a solo ride of 150 kilometres, finished fourteen minutes ahead of Lucien Teisseire, also a new name. Four weeks later the Tour of Flanders yielded a convincing solo victory for the young Rik van Steenbergen. He would have won anyway since he was an extraordinarily fast sprinter, but was keen to finish alone.

The Second World War lasted longer than the First, but that was certainly not the only reason why a new generation of racing cyclists were announcing themselves. The most important reason was that there was much more cycling activity between 1939 and 1945 than between 1914 and 1918. In France, the Netherlands, and Belgium, the military phase of the war was soon over, so that soldiers who had been conscripted were in service for only a short time. Some riders, like the Belgian Emile Masson, ended up in POW camps, but most were soon able to resume their profession. Many races were organised in the neutral countries, in the unoccupied part of France, and in Italy, but even the German-occupied countries had a reasonably full calendar. Major tours and long races like Paris–Brest–Paris and Bordeaux–Paris, and races that crossed borders, like Paris–Brussels, were cancelled, but other classics were held more than once. Indeed, the Tour of Flanders was held every year. The riders, of course, were mainly nationals of the country in question, but

Swiss and Belgian cyclists often participated in France, and Italians sometimes did as well.

The outbreak of war initially caused serious trouble for *L'Auto*. The number of sports events to be covered were so few that at the end of 1939 the editors decided to rename the paper *L'Auto-Soldat* and to start publishing war news. Only after France had capitulated and sports events recommenced did the journal resume its old name.

Henri Desgrange died in 1940. His successors tried to follow in his footsteps as much as possible, even though circulation sometimes dropped far below 100,000. They even announced a Tour de France in 1943, but the authorities would not give their consent to this plan.

The editors' attempts to ensure the survival of their newspaper were initially successful. Eventually, though, they turned out to be counterproductive. After liberation in 1944 *L'Auto* was proscribed, like all other newspapers that had appeared during the occupation. This meant the Tour de France was deprived of its organiser. Because of a shortage of paper, sports journals did not at first get permission to publish, and it was not until 1946 that the struggle over *L'Auto*'s legacy began in earnest. Three candidates presented themselves: *Elans*, *Sports*, and *L'Equipe*. For 1946 all three papers announced a mini-Tour of five stages, the maximum permitted by the government. Two of these actually did take place. The first was the *Ronde de France*, a race from Bordeaux to Grenoble, organised by *Sports* in cooperation with the daily newspaper *Le Soir*. *L'Equipe*, which had merged with *Elans*, launched a *Petit Tour de France*, which ran from Monaco to Paris. Victory in this race went to Jean 'Apo' Lazaridès, 'the Greek child', even though at one point he seemed to have passed up any chance of winning when he dropped back to the peloton after a lonely escape on the Izoard because he suddenly got worried about bears. Apparently the psychology of fear that Desgrange had sought to create on the eve of the first stage through the Pyrenees in 1910 could still claim a victim.

After much intrigue behind the scenes *L'Equipe*, in association with the general-interest newspaper *Le Parisien Libéré*, finally succeeded in getting control of the organisation of the Tour. The manager of *L'Equipe*, Jacques Goddet, who had been Desgrange's assistant before the war, became the new *patron* or boss of the Tour, while the sports editor-in-chief of *Le Parisien Libéré*, Félix Lévitan, was appointed assistant director. Although all kinds of necessary commodities, such as petrol for the team cars, were still being rationed, in 1947 Goddet and Lévitan decided to organise a revival of the Tour de France. The announcement aroused enormous public enthusiasm. The first post-war years were a drab period, with little remaining of the great expectations awakened by the liberation. In spite of American aid, there were shortages of everything, and bread rations that summer fell to their lowest level since 1944. The prospect of a Tour de France provided a welcome diversion, especially because no sports events of a similar scope had taken place since the end of the war. The story is told that the dock-workers threatened to go out on strike when the Minister of Supply hesitated to grant the Tour management's request to make the necessary quantities of food and petrol available.

x x x

Probably no other Tour has been followed by the French with more passion than the one of 1947. It was contested by national teams, of course, just as in the 1930s. Aside from these a number of French regional teams were entered, a new experiment that dated from 1939. The participants did not disappoint the public. The Italian federation declined to send an official team, as a consequence of which the two strongest cyclists at that time, Coppi and Bartali, did not appear at the start. But their absence failed to diminish interest in the Tour. On the contrary, the absence of stars with sufficient authority to control the race simply increased the tension. Furthermore, due to extremely hot weather and the inadequate preparation of most of the peloton, the progress of the race was extremely capricious, with constantly changing fortunes, monumental collapses, and sensational comebacks. Moreover, the journalists performed wonders by depicting the main contenders as eccentric personalities who gave rise to one picturesque anecdote after another. One was 'King' René Vietto, who maintained discipline in the peloton by slapping a rider who sought to escape across the face. The 'silent' Italian Aldo Ronconi – he spoke no French – was coached by his brother Don Silvio, who looked very odd as he ran after his brother at the end of each stage, his priest's soutane flapping about his legs. In the major Pyreneean stages, Don Silvio dressed himself as a mechanic to get around the rule prohibiting the presence of family members in the support caravan. Jean-Marie 'Ademaï' Goasmat, the first great cycling star of the radio era, heard his nickname change over the years from 'the elf' to 'the Breton gnome' and finally 'the cycling menhir'. It was said of Edouard Fachleitner, 'the shepherd from Manosque', that he phoned home every evening to speak with his dog, and that he lost the Tour because at some point he got fed up and stopped for half an hour to eat his lunch under a tree (in reality he was overcome by the heat, and his break lasted only ten minutes). When Pierre Brambilla, 'Lantern Jaw' as he was known, suffered from exhaustion, he shouted to himself that someone who rode so badly did not deserve to have a drink and emptied his water bottle – said to be filled with red wine – on the road. Finally, Jean Robic, who would collect more nicknames in the course of his career than any other rider, among them 'little goat' (*biquet*), 'glasshead', 'leatherhead' and 'the king of the Pyrenees', amused everyone by claiming from day one of the Tour that he was 'irresistible'.

Aside from all the colourful details to which the readers of *L'Equipe* and other papers were treated daily, the Tour offered the French public an extremely satisfying spectacle. For days on end it seemed as if René Vietto would at last be able to get his justified revenge on fate, which had ostensibly kept him from victory in 1934. When he lost the yellow jersey to Brambilla two days before the end a catastrophe loomed, but against all expectations Robic managed to set matters straight during the final stage. Italian journalists cried blue murder because Robic and his companion Fachleitner had been able to ride in the slipstream of photographers' motorcycles for many kilometres, but of course the French press did not mention this flagrant breach of the rules. They paid more attention to the story that, after his arrival in Paris, Brambilla drove home at once, chopped his bike into pieces, and buried them in the garden.

The Tour of 1947 inaugurated a period in which cycle racing reached the apex of its popularity. Every year hundreds of thousands of spectators lined the roads during the classics and the major tours in order to see the riders race past. The Tour and the Giro became festivals that lasted for three uninterrupted weeks. The liquor companies represented in the advertising caravan threw parties in each of the stage towns that went on into the early hours, with contributions from the most celebrated stars of the musical stage, such as Charles Trenet (Pernod) and Tino Rossi (Ricard) in the Tour, or Beniamino Gigli (Martini) in the Giro.

The most important development in racing during the years after the Second World War was that it became much more international than it had been in the 1930s. This was largely due to an initiative taken by the key sports journals in France, Italy, and Belgium, *L'Equipe*, *La Gazzetta dello Sport*, *Sportwereld*, and *Les Sports*. Their managements decided to offer an annual trophy to the rider who scored the best results in the nine most important races organised by their newspapers. This Desgrange-Colombo Challenge, named after the grand old men of French and Italian cycle sport, comprised the Tour, the Giro, Milan–San Remo, the Tour of Flanders, the Tour of Lombardy, the Flèche Wallonne, Paris–Tours, Paris–Roubaix, and Paris–Brussels. Because these nine races, to which Liège–Bastogne–Liège and the Tour of Switzerland were later added, were generally regarded as the most important of the cycling season (aside from the world championship) and received a lot of extra publicity in the journals that were sponsoring the trophy, the Challenge enjoyed greater prestige than the present-day World Cup of Cycling, which is limited to one-day races. It stimulated Italian teams, especially, to participate more frequently in foreign classics. The French manufacturers were less responsive: for them the Tour continued to be of overriding importance. All the same, many French riders participated in the Giro, Milan–San Remo, or the Tour of Lombardy. In these cases they normally signed a temporary contract with an Italian company. For example, Louison Bobet and Raphaël Géminiani rode in France for Stella and Métropole, but in Italy for Bottecchia and Bianchi. Their employers did not object, because at that time the markets for French and Italian bicycles barely overlapped.

Thanks to the Desgrange-Colombo Challenge, later succeeded by the Superprestige Pernod, the Belgian and Italian races included in the competition lost the almost exclusively national character they had previously had. No foreigner had ever succeeded in winning the Giro d'Italia or the Flèche Wallonne, and none had won the Tour of Lombardy since 1920. The Tour of Flanders had never had even one non-Flemish winner, while Milan–San Remo had, since 1913, seen a non-Italian victory only in 1934. All that now changed. In 1950 the Swiss Hugo Koblet won the Giro, a year later the Frenchman Louison Bobet triumphed in Milan–San Remo and the Tour of Lombardy. The Italians Fermo Camellini and Fausto Coppi won the Flèche Wallonne in 1948 and 1950 respectively, and Fiorenzo

Magni managed to win three straight Tours of Flanders, from 1949 through 1951. The Italian and Belgian fans were naturally not all that enthusiastic about these developments. When Magni won the Tour of Flanders for the third time in 1951 and the first Fleming finished in sixth place, twelve minutes back, Karel van Wijnendaele wrote that Belgian cycling fans had but one thing left: 'We still have our eyes to weep with.' But in the long run the stature of these races could only gain from foreign victories. A triumph in the Giro or a classic became even more desirable than it used to be, because now it was a victory over the best riders in the world.

The 1940s and 1950s were also a golden age for cycling journalism. Radio, film newsreels, and the first television broadcasts meant more publicity for road racing than ever before. At the same time they showed so little of the actual progress of the race that reporters had full scope to interpret it in their own individual way. Just as in the 1930s, some riders had a special talent for gaining more prominence in the newspaper reports and race commentary than they actually deserved on the basis of their achievements. One of them was Jean Robic, an excellent climber but too limited as a rider to be able to hold his own with the *campionissimi*. After the 1947 Tour he failed to score any further major triumphs, but he managed to compensate for this by presenting himself, with full conviction, as the victim of a malevolent outside world. His theatrical high point came in the longest Alpine stage in 1952, when he punctured on the climb to the finish in Sestriere. Because Robic's team director, Marcel Bidot, was driving behind Nello Laurédi, the highest-placed French National rider, there was no support car at hand. In those days riders always carried a spare tyre around their shoulders and Robic could have fixed the problem within two minutes. Instead, weeping and whining, he started pumping air into his tyre, which cost him a minute. And because this was obviously a very temporary measure, he soon had to get off his bike again to repeat the operation, and again and again, five times altogether, according to journalists (eight times according to Robic himself). And every time 'Biquet' called out with a tear-choked voice: 'Where is Bidot?' to drive home to those reporters who had not heard him the first time the point that he had been 'betrayed' by his team director.

x x x

72

There were so many authentic champions in those days that it was unnecessary to create pseudo-stars, and journalists took Robic seriously in his role as victim only as long as he produced appealing results. When in 1959, aged 38, he tried to make a comeback in the Tour, his complaints had become merely risible. That was tragic, because it was in this of all years that he deserved admiration for the way he was able to hold his own until three days before the end, in spite of a broken bone in one of his hands. He was like the boy who cried wolf once too often: no one believed him any more.

Riders like Robic were important to journalists in those days mainly as an inexhaustible source of diversion. Most of the attention, of course, went to the genuinely great riders of the time, men like Coppi, Bartali, Magni, Van Steenbergen, Bobet, Koblet, and Ferdi Kübler, men who, also partly because of the perfecting of the *domestique* system and the great differences in strength within the peloton, scored victories that inspired the journalists to their best prose.

At the centre stood the duels between the Italians Fausto Coppi and Gino Bartali, which took on such epic form that the Italian novelist Dino Buzzati, who covered the 1949 Giro as a specially-contracted reporter, spontaneously compared them to the Homeric struggle between Achilles and Hector. In the first Giro d'Italia in which both riders took part, that of 1940, Coppi was still one of Bartali's *domestiques*. The latter was the odds-on favourite that year, but a fall in the second stage left him hopelessly far behind while Coppi captured the pink jersey. Bartali wanted to quit the race, but his team director, Eberardo Pavesi, was able to convince him that he could, by helping Coppi, become even more popular than he already was. Nothing touches the public as much as a great star who renders service to a young, inexperienced member of his team. Bartali's 'sacrifice' did indeed earn him general admiration, but Coppi, who did not surrender the pink jersey for the remainder of the Giro, became a star through his victory.

Very soon the Italian newspapers sought to quicken the interest of their readers with tales about the ruthless rivalry that was supposed to exist between the two champions. In reality they still got along very well at that time. Nevertheless, their good relationship was inevitably affected by the continuing press campaigns and the expectations of the public. When Coppi switched to Bianchi in 1946 while Bartali stayed with Legnano, the 'real' conflict began.

This soon took on dimensions that far exceeded the bounds of cycle sport. The writer Curzio Malaparte was of the opinion that no Italian could avoid taking sides; in his view the fight between Coppi and Bartali divided the country in two. This indicates that the rivalry between the two champions touched on much more fundamental issues than purely sporting ones. Coppi and Bartali were regarded as incarnations of the contrasts that marked Italy in the post-war years. Bartali, the Christian Democrat, stood for traditional Italy and Catholicism; Coppi personified modernism, cool rationalism, and socialism.

It was an image that squared only very imperfectly with reality, even though it was quite true that the two champions differed strongly from each other in more than one respect. For example, Coppi differentiated himself from his rival by his 'modern' approach to cycling. Whereas Bartali was a rider in the old mould, who never thought for a moment of giving up his daily litre of red wine or his packet of cigarettes, Coppi experimented with technical improvements, advanced methods of nutrition, and new chemical supplements. And there was not a shadow of a doubt that Bartali was a strong believer. He was active in *Azione Cattolica* and a member of the third order of the Carthusians. While riding he carried five or six medallions of the Holy Virgin or Saint Theresa of Lisieux around his neck and across his handlebars. On one occasion, the start of a stage in the Tour de France had to be delayed because Bartali had taken his entire team to church and stayed there praying for a good hour and a half. Moreover, he maintained close ties with Alcide de Gasperi, leader of the Christian Democratic party. But Coppi did not necessarily belong in the other camp where religion was concerned. He said he was a good Catholic, and together with Bartali and several other well-known Italians, urged people to vote 'patriotic' in the elections of 1948, which meant for the Christian Democrats and against the Popular Front. Statements and gestures of this kind barely produced any change in the image that had formed around the two riders. The sharp social and political contrasts that dominated Italian life in the 1940s and 1950s led almost everything to be seen in terms of thesis and antithesis. Because Bartali was very devout, in the eyes of most Italians Coppi just had to be an agnostic or an atheist. Even Coppi's audience with the Pope after his victory in the 1947 Giro could not change this: at once rumours began to circulate that he had gone to the Vatican with considerable reluctance.

The first few years after the Second World War constituted the high point in the rivalry between the two *campionissimi*. In 1946 and 1947 there was little to choose between the two. Each won the Giro d'Italia and Milan–San Remo once. In spite of his 34 years, Bartali was able to trump his rival in 1948 by scoring one of the most startling Tour victories in history. At the foot of the Alps he was more than 21 minutes behind the wearer of the yellow jersey, Louison Bobet, who had administered a crushing defeat to him the day before. The majority of the journalists were convinced that Bartali had 'written his last page as champion'. The opposite turned out to be the case. Bartali won the next three Alpine stages with a display of overwhelming power, and when the mountains lay behind Bartali had a 32 minute lead on the second-placed rider. As if this were not enough, the myth arose that with his sensational victory Bartali had saved his country from civil war. The day after the stage in which Bobet crushed him, the secretary of the Italian Communist party, Palmiro Togliatti, was seriously wounded in an attempt on his life. Prime Minister De Gasperi, the story goes, was of the view that a civil war was almost inevitable and saw but one way out. Only a Bartali victory in the Tour could settle people down. He made an urgent telephone call to the champion and explained the situation to him. Conscious of the mission assigned to him, Bartali smashed his opponents and saved the country. It mattered little that the moment of greatest danger had already passed by the time the Prime Minister phoned. When Bartali returned to Italy he was welcomed as the 'saviour of his country'. 'The sun goes down, but not Bartali,' his supporters wrote with whitewash on walls and road surfaces.

How could Coppi compete with a man like that? Bartali was so popular that he did not need to do anything to please his fans. He never blamed his team-mates for any mishap, but always and everywhere he complained about the rest of the world. Nor was he always all that friendly to his competitors. Once when Hugo Koblet asked him for his water bottle, Bartali emptied it before handing it over. Upon arrival he often made a disagreeable face, even if he had won, and pushed the enthusiastic fans roughly out of his way. But love does not need to be requited in order to flourish. Most Italians adored Bartali, whereas Coppi excited admiration rather than passion. His legend flowered fully only after his death, and for a long time it was cherished abroad to a greater degree than in Italy itself.

After his great year in 1948, Bartali was clearly outstripped by Coppi. But that scarcely lessened his popularity. Even after Coppi beat him badly in the 1949 Giro, fully 70 per cent of Italians still preferred Bartali. Besides, he was often able to take the sting out of Coppi's victories in a very crafty way. He provided a fine example of this in the 1949 Tour, when both were members of the Italian national squad. At the foot of the Alps, each of them was so far behind the leaders on general classification that an Italian victory had become doubtful. On the urging of team director Alfredo Binda, the two men agreed to help each other as much as possible in the mountain stages to come. This tactic was successful. Two days later, after ascending the last col of the day, the Petit Saint Bernard, they occupied the top two positions overall: Bartali in the yellow jersey and Coppi in second place. And yet Bartali knew he had already lost the Tour. Coppi had not experienced a single moment's difficulty in the mountains and on general classification he was less than a minute and a half back. Because he was a far better *rouleur* than his rival, no one doubted he would erase this difference without much trouble in the 137-kilometre time trial that was soon to come. Bartali was in danger of losing the Tour in humiliating fashion when, 40 kilometres from the finish in Aosta, he punctured and soon afterwards came off his bike. This could not have happened at a better time. To show he was keeping his end of the bargain, Coppi stopped pedalling and freewheeled until Binda gave him the order to go on by himself. From that moment on Coppi held nothing back and arrived in Aosta with a lead of almost five minutes, so that the yellow jersey passed from Bartali to him. After this, Bartali was able to pretend that victory in the Tour had escaped him because of bad luck, and that he had not been beaten on merit. In fact, he milked even more credit from the situation. Immediately upon finishing he declared: 'When my tyre went flat, my first thought was: Italy! Perhaps Robic, Marinelli and Lazaridès would have regained courage if they had heard that we were held up by misfortune. And the most important thing was that an Italian should win in Italy. So I said to Fausto that he must go on as fast as he could.'

Coppi was five years younger than his rival, but that made it all the harder to win the favour of the public. In 1948 Bartali had already reached an age at which most racing cyclists have retired. It seemed only natural for Coppi to beat him. On the other hand, if Bartali won, his ecstatic fans regarded it as a miracle. When he won the

Tour of Emilia on 1 May 1952, the staff of the sports paper *Stadio* decided to give up their day off so that an extra edition with news of their idol's triumph could appear the next day.

No wonder Coppi never felt a moment's ease when he had to ride a race in which Bartali was also competing. During the years he had to put up with Bartali as a team-mate, Coppi never succeeded in becoming world champion. Only in 1953 did the road open up for him: Bartali, to his great annoyance, was not selected for the Italian team. Nevertheless he tried to hinder his rival by means of a symbolic presence: he arranged to have billboards placed along the circuit carrying advertisements for Bartali bicycles and Bartali wine in bold letters. It no longer had an effect. Coppi crossed the finish line in first place with a five-minute lead.

In 1949 Coppi and Bartali stood head and shoulders above the other riders in the Tour. A year later they were in danger of dropping to the second tier because of the meteoric rise of a new idol, the Swiss Hugo Koblet, who, in 1950, became the first non-Italian to win the Giro. Koblet was far from plain looking and the cycling press, which always examines the qualities of champions through a magnifying glass, at once proclaimed him to be 'as beautiful as a god'. He paid as much attention to his appearance as Charles Pélissier and always carried a pocket comb so he could tidy his hair on his arrival at the finish line, something even 'Beau Brummel' never thought of. But Koblet *was* a much better rider than Pélissier. The absolute high point of his cycling career came in 1951, when he won the Tour with a 22-minute lead, and with his achievement in the eleventh stage between Brive and Agen seemed to raise himself above the natural laws of cycle racing. Everyone knows that on flat roads a lone cyclist does not have a ghost of a chance against an unleashed peloton. Yet Koblet, and this in spite of being among *the* great favourites to win the Tour, rode solo for 135 kilometres and crossed the finish with a two-and-a-half minute lead. 'That kind of thing just doesn't happen,' Tim Krabbé writes in his masterpiece *The Rider,* 'nothing like Brive-Agen had ever happened before, and it has never happened again.'

Obviously the journalists were transported into raptures of admiration and sought to excel each other in the superlatives they used. In the *Miroir du Cyclisme* Abel Michéa referred to Koblet as 'no longer human but a hero, a sort of demigod'. One of Michéa's colleagues wrote about 'an eagle pursued by a pack of jackals', which was not only a new metaphor but a zoological novelty. *L'Equipe*'s Pierre About was prepared to concede that a few drops of sweat had been visible on Koblet's forehead – handsome Hugo always carried a sponge to wipe them off at the finish line – but that they did not smell unpleasant, because 'the sweat of the gods contains no urea'!

Perhaps not, but was Koblet in fact a god? From the film clips of that day it would seem he was. They show a smoothly-riding Koblet, hands on the tops of his handlebars and protective goggles around his upper arm, alternating with chaotic images of the pursuing group. The commentary: 'Because of the high speed of the chase, the peloton breaks into pieces.'

From the printed stage results it is evident that the peloton actually crossed the finish line in close formation. And if you study the journal images closely, you will notice several men with white crosses on their jerseys riding at the front: Swiss riders, Koblet's team-mates trying to slow down the tempo. This suggests that the vanguard of the peloton made a chaotic impression not because the speed was insanely high but because the pursuit was badly organised. This is confirmed by an incident that took place during Koblet's solo ride: the leading Frenchman, Louison Bobet, was delayed for three minutes by mechanical trouble, but, nevertheless, with the aid of two *domestiques*, he was able to rejoin the peloton in relatively short order. Before he had done so, of course, his team-mates did not participate in the pursuit of Koblet. And the Italians, in any case divided because of the presence of Coppi, Bartali and Magni in the same team, had scant desire to do the heavy lifting by themselves. The notion that Koblet held out by himself for three hours against an all-out chase by the peloton is a fable. The over-all tempo during the stage was fairly high, but only in its final phase was the peloton in really hot pursuit. As a result Koblet lost part of his lead. That takes nothing away from his achievement – a lesser rider would surely have been caught – but the circumstances clearly favoured him. His victory in Brive-Agen is rightly counted among the high points of the history of cycle racing. It undoubtedly ranks with the finest victories of Coppi or Eddie Merckx, but not above them.

x x x

The myth of Koblet's superhuman capacities was created by journalists who wanted to dish up a good story for their readers and saw the *pédaleur de charme* as an ideal star. The riders who had been beaten by Koblet knew better, of course, but they had no interest in protesting. Not only because it would have painted them as bad losers, but also because they had little reason to be proud of themselves. When a favourite in a major race is so overconfident that he escapes by himself long before the finish, the standard tactic is simply to let him go, leave him to 'swim' by himself as long as possible, and reel him in just before the end. For the riders who carried out only the first two parts of this programme, the idea that Koblet commanded supernatural powers that day must have presented a splendid excuse.

Not only in the short, but also in the long run, riders could only gain from the persistence of legends of this kind. Until well into the 1980s appearance fees in criteriums and kermesses were the chief sources of income for professionals, and without the myth of the giants of the road these fees would have been a good deal lower. The public turned out mainly to see the stars, and quite naturally they earned by far the most money. After his 1952 Tour victory Coppi received contracts totalling more than 20 million francs, certainly a fortune in those days. Second-tier riders could also profit handsomely from the glory of the great champions. For example, Jan Nolten was idolised in the Netherlands after the 1952 Tour. When he appeared at the start of a criterium, people crowded around just to be able to touch his bike. This happened only in small part because he had won a stage. Far more important was that he had duelled with Coppi as they climbed the Puy de Dôme together and had lost only narrowly. Moreover, the *campionissimo*, interviewed on Dutch radio, had given him a patent of cycling nobility by predicting a great future for him.

It is therefore not surprising that riders who were in close proximity to 'the giants of the road' often actively contributed to their legendary status, basking in its reflected glory. Many of the tall tales about Coppi originated with his former team-mate Raphaël Géminiani who, for many years after his retirement, profited as team director and TV-announcer from the reputation he had built up as a rider. Here, for example, is his account of Coppi's decisive breakaway on the slope of the Crespera during the 1953 world championships in Lugano:

I saw him pull away like a rocket with his 47 by 21. I really did try to react and I actually managed to get to within a few metres of his wheel. But Fausto resumed his charge with prodigious strength. He passed the entire group and within half a kilometre left Bobet and me 200 metres behind. It was perhaps the greatest surprise of my career. I've never seen anything like it again…

What Géminiani does not say is that the Belgian Germain Derijcke stayed smartly on Coppi's wheel during all this and did not allow himself to be shaken off during the next five ascents of the Crespera either. That happened only when the *campionissimo*, who was beginning to worry about the toughness shown by his companion, offered him a huge sum of money to drop back. Anyway, even without this offer Coppi would have won, because Derijcke was so exhausted that he lost more than six minutes during the remaining ten kilometres.

Louison Bobet contributed his bit to the Coppi legend as well, by claiming that, with Coppi's appearance on the scene, the average speed of bicycle races rose from 32 to 40 or even 42 kilometres per hour. It is easy to demonstrate that this is nonsense. In 1938, when Coppi was still racing with the juniors, the yellow pennant, the prize awarded for a classic victory with the highest average speed, was held by the Italian Jules Rossi, who won Paris–Tours that year with an average speed of 42.1 km/h. At the end of Coppi's career, twenty years later, the record stood at 43.8 km/h. The average speed of Milan–San Remo rose in that period from 38.5 to 40.3 km/h. Average speeds in the Tour actually fell after Coppi's appearance on the scene, because he had his *domestiques* control the race to such an extent that battles which would have stepped up the pace could not break out. The record average at the time belonged to Bartali with 33.4; the average in the three Tours in which Coppi took part fluctuated between 31.4 and 32.1 km/h.

All the same, this myth, too, has proved extraordinarily durable. This is not at all strange: tales like this continue to form one of the main elements of cycle racing's appeal to the public. They are launched by journalists, confirmed by riders, and acquiesced in by manufacturers. The interests of the main parties often diverge, but this myth, as Jacques Calvet writes in *Le mythe des géants de la route*, is a phenomenon from which all three can exact a profit.

7

Pens in a Trance, Lenses in Delirium

The golden age of cycle sport after the Second World War was initially also a golden age for the bicycle industry. In France, 1949 was the year not only of the immortal duels between Coppi and Bartali in the Tour, but also of a sales record of 1,300,000 bicycles, some 300,000 more than in 1938, the top pre-war year.

Starting in 1950, sales figures began to fall. In 1951 they dropped below a million, a year later to 750,000. A temporary low point was reached in 1957 with sales of 534,000. This decline had nothing to do with the accomplishments of Coppi's successors or the popularity of the Tour de France. It was caused by another phenomenon altogether: the rise of the moped. In 1948 French factories turned out fewer than 40,000 of these; by 1956 the number had already risen to more than 900,000.

Most bicycle manufacturers did not command sufficient capital and expertise to capture a segment of this new market. Many of them got into serious trouble as a result. Several firms had to close their doors, and just as in the early 1930s, only a few of them were willing or able to finance a team of cyclists.

The Italian rider Fiorenzo Magni, a man who showed both before and after the end of his cycling career that he had great business savvy, was the first to find a solution to this perilous state of affairs. When his employer Luigi Ganna (winner of the first Giro) announced that he would dissolve his team at the end of the 1953 season, Magni went searching for a new sponsor. He knew it was pointless to approach other cycle manufacturers and therefore contacted firms without any connection to the bicycle industry. He succeeded in securing several provisional pledges, and in February 1954 he called a meeting of Italian professional riders to get support for his plans. Coppi and Bartali, the only two whose opinion really mattered, both agreed, and after the Italian cycling federation had also given its approval, at the start of the 1954 season Magni presented a team whose jerseys carried the word Nivea instead of the name of a bicycle firm. Gino Bartali followed Magni's example and concluded an agreement with the raincoat manufacturer Brooklyn, which would act as co-sponsor with his own bicycle company.

Magni's idea was not altogether new. Some years earlier Spanish riders had begun to carry advertising for *extra-sportif* businesses on their jerseys. Since, on political grounds, cycle sport in Franco's Spain had been relatively isolated for years, the *Union Cycliste Internationale* (UCI) had never paid much attention to it. Now that this development had reached a classic cycling nation like Italy, it could no longer be ignored. Jacques Goddet fulminated against the new development because he was of the opinion – quite rightly – that the world of cycling would thereby surrender a part of its autonomy. The UCI adopted a motion of disapproval, and the French association even went so far as to ban riders who went to work for an *extra-sportif* firm from races in France. When Bartali appeared at the start line of the Mont Faron climb in the spring of 1954, he was allowed to begin only after paying a 25,000-lire fine. To forestall difficulties, the Italian federation decided not to send a team to the Tour de France that year.

The economic situation soon forced Tour officials to change their stance. By the end of 1954 it became clear that the French bicycle industry did not command sufficient resources to give employment to the whole body of French professional cyclists. Even successful riders such as Jean Dotto, fourth in the 1954 Tour, and Nello Laurédi, three-time winner of the Dauphiné Libéré, failed to find sponsors. Raphaël Géminiani, who had given his name to a make of bicycle, decided to break the impasse. He concluded an agreement with the Saint-Raphaël apéritif company, and in the spring of 1955 he presented the Saint-Raphaël Géminiani team, a name that must have given him a lot of pleasure, because he was far from being a saint. To save face, the French cycling authorities reprimanded Géminiani, but they did not otherwise block him. A year later the great majority of professional cyclists were riding on behalf of *extra-sportif* firms, although in France these were allowed to act only as co-sponsors.

This revolution took place so quickly because it dovetailed with another new development: the coming of television. At the outset, cycle sport profited but little from this. The first regular televised broadcasts of races took place in 1952, but these were just reports from the finish line that were over in a flash. Only after the development of the system whereby a television camera was connected via helicopter directly with the studio, a procedure first used during Paris–Roubaix in 1960, was it possible to show more of the progress of a race. In the meantime the popularity of bicycle racing had already been significantly eroded by the rise of sports that lent themselves more easily to television coverage. Football in particular benefited from the new medium. Especially after the creation of the European Cup in the 1955-56 season – an initiative of *L'Equipe* – and the television coverage of the 1958 World Cup, won by the appealing Brazilian wonder team of Pelé, Didi, and Garrincha, football became outstandingly popular as a television spectator sport.

Interest in bicycle racing continued, but it had lost its position as *the* media sport. That was also the reason why the *monstres sacrés*, the superstars of the first post-war decade when cycle sport occupied a unique place, did not seem to have real successors. To be sure, Charly Gaul, 'the Angel of the Mountains', Federico Bahamontes, 'the Eagle of Toledo', Gastone Nencini, 'the Mugello lion', Miguel Poblet, 'the divine baldhead', and Rik van Looy, 'the Emperor of Herentals', had nicknames as fine as their predecessors, but they lacked the aura of divinity that emanated from Coppi, Bartali, and Koblet.

From the end of the 1950s, cycle racing occupied a clearly less central position in the media than before, but for the business world it remained the key sport for a long time. The links between commerce and football were still so weak that it took years before sponsorships and company advertising on jerseys became accepted phenomena. Professional cyclists, on the other hand, had been carrying company names on their jerseys for decades, a *fait accompli* accepted even by the Dutch television authorities – in commercial matters the puritans of Europe. And although the TV broadcasts of the 1950s were fairly primitive, the company names were clearly visible. For the time being that was good enough for the *extra-sportif* sponsors.

It is customary to measure the success of cycling teams by the number of victories they score. Yet for *extra-sportif* firms these are at most a means of gaining publicity, and not an end in themselves. Riders who rode for bicycle companies had to demonstrate by their achievements the quality of the equipment they used. When Coppi beat Bartali, the implication was that a Bianchi bike was better than a Legnano, that a Campagnolo derailleur worked more efficiently than a Vittoria, and that Ursus made faster and more reliable tyres than Pirelli. When a rider riding for an *extra-sportif* brand gains a victory, a credible connection between achievement and product can rarely be established. Simmons did have the sprinter André Darrigade make the claim that he owed his win to the superbly restful nights he enjoyed on the company's mattresses, but that was an exception. Nobody would ever have believed that Fiorenzo Magni won the Giro because he rubbed Nivea into his skin, that Gastone Nencini became king of the mountains because he brushed his teeth with Chlorodont, or that Charly Gaul owed his climbing abilities to espresso made with a Faema coffee maker. What the *extra-sportif* sponsors desired from their cyclists was good publicity and a positive image. These could be achieved by winning races, but that was certainly not the only way. A spectacular defeat, beautifully captured in pictures, was much more valuable than an unobtrusive victory. The dramatic break in Eugène Christophe's front fork was a publicity disaster for the Peugeot bicycle company; for an *extra-sportif* brand the incident would have been heaven-sent.

In the days when teams were employed by bicycle firms, the commercial value of the riders was principally determined by the number of victories they gained. It did not matter if, during an interview, they had nothing to say. Antonin Magne rarely opened his mouth, but the sole consequence was that he was called 'the Silent', which lent his image an extra dimension. Something different was expected from riders sponsored by an *extra-sportif* company. If they were incapable of holding their own conversationally when faced with a microphone, they fell short in their duty to their employer, because that meant television reporters rarely found it worthwhile to push a microphone at them after the end of a race, the moment at which a brand name appeared most conspicuously in the picture. Men like the Dutchman Gerrie Knetemann, who after six hours of racing was just as well-spoken as before the start, or his compatriot Gerben Karstens, who managed to name his sponsor at least once in every interview, were worth their weight in gold to their companies. For a time Vittorio Adorni was the best-paid cyclist in Italy, not because of his victories but because he developed into a charismatic television personality, who, as soon as he had crossed the finish line, was able to analyse the course of the race with lucidity and humour. The '*Ciao, mamma!*' with which he ended every interview was so famous that it became the title of a show Adorni hosted on Italian television while he was still cycling. As a result of these activities, his on-camera performance became more important than his racing feats. The story goes that he once fell back from the winning position just before the end of an Italian semi-classic because he sensed he was too exhausted to come up with his usual sparkling post-finish patter.

In the 1950s there were only a few riders who could meet the demands of the television era. Most professional racing cyclists of that time came from a poverty-stricken agrarian milieu and lacked the background or education to act as PR representatives. The bicycle manufacturers for whom they used to work had never cared about that, but the managers of the *extra-sportif* companies required their cyclists to move as easily in the larger world as in a bicycle race. Especially in the presence of journalists they were supposed to behave and dress appropriately. When the Belgian Fred De Bruyne was placed on contract by the Carpano vermouth company in 1957, he not only became acquainted with new training methods, but also received lessons in Italian and etiquette.

As TV came to play a greater role, the *extra-sportif* brands proved ready to invest ever larger amounts in their teams. Not only did the stars get much higher salaries than their predecessors, but so did the riders surrounding them. The result was that team discipline became much stricter than it had been. To a certain extent the team-mates of Kübler, Bobet, or Van Steenbergen had the freedom to ride for themselves. Coppi was the first champion to surround himself with *domestiques* who rode only to serve his needs. Generally these were the sons of poor farm labourers who made fairly modest financial demands and had learned from an early age to accommodate themselves to the wishes of their social betters. They were prepared to negate themselves completely for the sake of their leader, and won a stage only when they had received specific authorisation to do so. On one occasion in the 1952 Tour one of these *gregari*, Andrea Carrea, took over the yellow jersey totally unexpectedly after he had joined an escape in order to slow down the pace. It should have been every rider's dream, but Carrea got the fright of his life. Imagine that his master might suspect him of nursing personal ambitions! The first thing Carrea did, after he donned the yellow jersey with obvious unhappiness, was to assure Coppi that there had been absolutely no intention involved. Only after the *campionissimo* had accepted Carrea's apologies did the new leader regain his composure.

As living standards rose, *domestiques* of this kind became ever rarer. From the 1960s on, the stars were often surrounded by team-mates who, despite impressive credentials, were unwilling or unable to carry the responsibility of being team leader and therefore undertook to serve a great champion. Thus Jacques Anquetil enjoyed the services of cyclists like Jean Stablinski, Rudi Altig, Louis Rostollan, Jo de Roo, and Ab Geldermans, who had won fine victories in their own right but would, when the need arose, show the same devotion to *their* leader as Coppi's *gregari* did to him. The same thing applied to the famous 'Red Brigade', the Faema team led by Rik van Looy, who was assisted by the likes of Raymond Impanis, Jos Hoevenaers, Noël Foré, Gilbert Desmet, Peter Post, and Jef Planckaert, each of whom had won one or more of the classics.

It goes without saying that riders of this stature were willing to surrender their own ambitions only when they were compensated financially. For this, an ample budget was needed, and because the managers of the *extra-sportif* companies were prepared to make this available only if they got the maximum return, they were ever less inclined to allow their riders to participate in the Tour de France, which was still contested by national teams. The consequence was that from 1957 to 1961 the Giro d'Italia could boast a stronger field of riders than the Tour and seemed to be developing into the premier stage-race. The world champion in 1960 and 1961, Rik van Looy, took part in the Giro three times in those years but made no appearance in the Tour de France. To make matters worse, the Tours of 1959, 1960, and 1961 provided very little excitement, so that public interest began to decline noticeably.

In 1962, the year French television announced that it would start televising live on a daily basis, pressure from the brand-name companies became so great that Tour directors Jacques Goddet and Félix Lévitan had to accept the inevitable: from that moment on the Tour would once again be contested by company teams.

Goddet and Lévitan did not take their decision out of full conviction. Just like Desgrange, they favoured the national format in principle because it tied in better with the chauvinism of sports fans and usually led to a more lively race. For *L'Auto* that had been an economic necessity because only in this way could enough papers be sold. But now that the additional circulation of the sponsoring newspapers yielded an ever smaller share of the enormous amount needed to organise the Tour, the contributions of the business firms that spent large sums of money for the right to sponsor one or other of the special classifications had become absolutely essential.

That was not, in fact, the reason Goddet and Lévitan gave for their decision. To preserve the image of bicycle racing as a pure test of strength, riders, organisers, and most cycling journalists had long observed the code of translating every motive into sporting terms. The Tour directors justified their decision to introduce the brand-name format not by referring to economic conditions, but by pointing instead to the difficulties that had arisen within the 1959 French team when it brought together several stars, and to the handicap the national format imposed on small countries such as Luxembourg.

This, of course, failed to pull the wool over anyone's eyes. In the Netherlands the transmissions offered by French television were refused in protest against the 'commercialisation' of the Tour. The broadcasting authorities went so far as to drop even radio broadcasts of the Tour and instead to offer coverage of the finish of stages in the *Tour de l'Avenir*, which was contested by amateurs. In France the popularity of the Tour sagged as well. This was partly a result of the nature of the race at the time. For several years the Tour was dominated by Jacques Anquetil, a great champion who had but one weakness: he scored victories without drama. Anquetil did not suffer from spectacular *défaillances*, undertook no long solo escapes, and made no unexpected comebacks. Seen from the technical and tactical points of view, his Tour victories were masterpieces, but they were unable to inspire much enthusiasm in the media and among the public. In 1961 he took the yellow jersey on the first day, at once taking an eight-minute lead on the other favourites. From that point on, aided by the strong French team, he succeeded in virtually immobilising the race. The superiority he demonstrated was so overwhelming that after the first mountain stage no one undertook any further serious effort to push him out of first place. Since Anquetil himself exhibited very little in the way of initiative, there was soon little for the journalists to say, other than that it was all rather tedious and boring. The public, which during one of the first live transmissions ever made watched the peloton pass in a tight bunch over the legendary cols of the Pyrenees, felt themselves cheated, and when Anquetil rode his victory lap through the Parc des Princes the spectators whistled loudly in disgust.

Anquetil never forgave the sportswriters for the whistling concert after his Tour victory. As he saw it, they had completely misinformed their readers. Instead of looking for cheap sensationalism they should have assessed his achievement for its proper value and should have made clear how hard it was to keep a peloton of 120 riders under control, how much energy it cost to remain vigilant for 21 stages, and how unique it was to carry the burden of a yellow jersey for the entire length of a Tour. According to Anquetil, cycling journalists had to give a realistic account of the progress of the race. This was in his view possible only if they described the course 'from inside out', or in other words, from the point of view of the cyclists. Later he put these opinions into practice himself, when, after the conclusion of his career, he contributed an extraordinarily candid question-and-answer column to *L'Equipe* while the Tour was on, often directly contradicting the opinions that were to be found elsewhere in the paper.

Of course Anquetil could not singlehandedly change the traditional method of reportage. The sportswriters generally tried to give an account of the race that was attuned as closely as possible to the tastes of their readership, even if this forced them to do violence to the truth – insofar as they were aware of it. In the journalists' eyes, the riders' only task was to provide the elements from which *they* could assemble the exciting stories on which the popularity of cycle sport was based.

Anquetil is perhaps the only great rider who never accepted the principles of this division of labour between journalists and riders. He wanted his occupation, professional bicycle racing, to be taken seriously and therefore consistently set his face against the false romanticism that enveloped it. He never sought to conform to the image of the cycling star that journalists so dearly loved to sketch, no matter how much advantage he could personally have derived from it. Thus he often stated that he had no special love of cycling and had become a racing cyclist solely to earn money; if he weren't paid for it, he said, he wouldn't ride even a single metre. As well as that, he was the only rider who declared, even while still active, that a professional rider had the right to look after himself as he thought best, even if he had to resort to methods that were regarded as doping.

Remarks of this kind certainly did nothing for his popularity. At first, in the early 1960s, he suffered little difficulty from this. His dominance as a tour rider was so great that he was indispensable in criteriums. The king of classics, Rik van Looy, was too weak as a climber and time trialist to threaten Anquetil in the Tour, and the only man from whom he had anything to fear in the mountains, Federico Bahamontes, 'the Eagle of Toledo', was already well into his thirties.

Most sportswriters did not quite know what to do with Anquetil's victories and would have greatly preferred a more popular champion. They believed they had found him in the person of Raymond Poulidor. In 1961 he won impressively in Milan–San Remo, and the following year he showed he was able to undertake successful solo rides in mountain stages, something Anquetil never risked doing. The journalists regarded Poulidor as the Messiah. They immediately proclaimed 'Poupou' to be a new Bartali and credited him with qualities that in their view the calculating Anquetil lacked: daring, combativeness, and generosity. Poulidor would finish in third place that year, but in the Parc des Princes the ovation he received was at least as loud as that given to Anquetil, who was quite understandably little pleased by this.

Soon the relationship between the two developed into a conflict that, like the rivalry between Coppi and Bartali, extended far beyond the boundaries of cycle sport. Due to the cool rationalism ascribed to him, Anquetil appeared as the incarnation of modern France; Poulidor represented the warmer traditionalism of *la France profonde*. Yet the parallel with the Italian *campionissimi* was only partly valid. Whereas Coppi and Bartali were equals for years, Poulidor was a much less impressive cyclist than Anquetil, and never succeeded in defeating his rival in a really important race. That did not hinder journalists from putting the two riders at the same level. Poulidor's continuing losses did not detract from this: these were invariably blamed on mechanical failure or, in the pompous manner of most race reports, 'ineluctable fate'.

Bad luck was too simple an explanation for Poulidor's defeats. In cycle sport bad luck is seldom coincidental. Of course it can happen that a rider falls or has trouble with his bike without being in any way at fault. The motorcyclists who move like kamikaze pilots through the peloton have caused many accidents that can hardly be blamed on the riders. In 1968 Poulidor, too, became the victim of a collision of this kind. With punctures and numerous other defects, such as broken forks, matters are less simple. Racing cyclists ride many thousands of kilometres annually, and if one falls more frequently or has more flat tyres than another, this cannot be coincidence. It is a well-known phenomenon that a good cyclist rarely has mechanical breakdowns. His concentration is better, he rides more smoothly, and he therefore places fewer demands on his equipment. For years Roger De Vlaeminck, 'Mr Paris–Roubaix', managed to avoid spills and punctures in 'the hell of the North'. His long spell of 'good luck' came to an end only when he began to lose his smooth pace over the cobblestones. Fausto Coppi, too, initially had the reputation of being immune to equipment failure and spills. After he turned 30 when cycling was bound to make heavier demands on him, he broke almost everything that could be broken. The unlucky devils in the peloton are often those riders who are trying to exceed their potential, like Jean Robic, who in his time was the absolute record holder where falls, breakages, and punctures were concerned.

That Anquetil did indeed suffer fewer mechanical problems than his rival was due to merit. Yet journalists were rarely inclined to take this into account in their comments on the Poulidor phenomenon. In the 1964 Tour 'Poupou' finished 55 seconds behind Anquetil yet simultaneously became by far the most popular rider in France. In practically every newspaper one could read that he, just like René Vietto 30 years earlier, was the 'moral victor' of the Tour because a crash had cost him more than two minutes. Not mentioned, of course, was that Anquetil would have followed a different tactic had his rival not been hit by this piece of 'bad luck'. Like all great champions, Anquetil had the ability to rise above himself. He won many races by a narrow margin; when he lost he always lagged well behind.

Moral victories are often more impressive than the real thing, and in 1964 Poulidor received more contracts for criteriums than Anquetil. The latter found it hard to accept that his five victories in the Tour and two triumphs in the Giro evidently counted for less than Poulidor's second place and his flat tyres. In contrast with the rivalry between Coppi and Bartali, on this occasion the press did not need to create any artificial hostility. Although the two French champions later became really good friends, during their careers they sincerely loathed each other. Anquetil, in particular, openly expressed himself in very unfriendly terms about his opponent. He stated in an interview that he found Poulidor to be 'uninteresting' as a person and did not consider him to be a genuine rival as a rider. In his opinion, the only one who qualified for this status was Rik van Looy. And when Poulidor promised, at the time the French team for the world championship (which was contested by national teams) was being assembled, that he would assist Anquetil if necessary, the latter reacted by saying that Poulidor 'was even more stupid than he had thought'.

Anquetil understood, of course, that he could not exorcise the spirit of Poulidor with words alone. He therefore made a serious attempt to shed his unsympathetic and calculating reputation. Together with his team director, Raphaël Géminiani, he settled on an insane enterprise intended to convince the public that he really *was* prepared to put himself out quite gratuitously. In 1965, immediately after his victory in the eight-stage Dauphiné Libéré, he took an aeroplane to Bordeaux, slept for an hour, and at 1:30 am appeared at the start of the 557-kilometre monster race from Bordeaux to Paris. Fifteen hours later he reached the finish, again as the winner. At last he had given the sportswriters the story they had long been waiting for. The popularity of Anquetil, 'champion of the impossible', did indeed grow. But less than that of Poulidor, who for the second straight year was beaten in the Tour by a small margin and in doing so created a new legend, that of 'the eternal runner-up'.

No wonder that Anquetil's behaviour began to show neurotic traits. In the 1966 Giro a modest rookie was flabbergasted to notice that one of Anquetil's *domestiques* was constantly shadowing him. When he inquired as to the reason, he was told his name was against him. It was Polidori. Not quite the same as Poulidor, but Anquetil clearly wanted to take no more chances.

'As an experiment' the 1967 Tour was once again contested according to the national formula. Because Anquetil did not enter, Poulidor was the undisputed leader of the French team, until the eighth stage, when he suffered such a *défaillance* during the ascent of the Ballon d'Alsace that he lost any chance of overall victory. For Anquetil, who owed his reputation to his achievements, this would have been a disaster. But not for Poulidor. He saw an opportunity to add significantly to his popularity by making himself useful to a *domestique*, just as Bartali had done in the 1940 Giro. The yellow jersey was on the back of the young French national rider Roger Pingeon (second place was held by Giancarlo Polidori!), and

Poulidor announced that during the rest of the Tour he would assist his team-mate as much as possible. The opportunity to make this promise good came in the key Alpine stage. When Poulidor had been dropped by the Italian Felice Gimondi (winner of the 1965 Tour) and the Spaniard Julio Jiménez, he fell back in order to tow Pingeon along. Wholly in accordance with the traditional prescription in such cases, Poulidor did not allow his team-mate to take the lead even for a metre. The journalists were in ecstasy:

> Pens go into a trance. Lenses are delirious and cameras are losing their heads. Poupou, the great Poupou, our national Poupou, in the service of the little plumber from Bugey! The air is alive with emotion, the pages of the notebooks become tri-coloured. What does it matter if Gimondi catches up with Jiménez, if Lucien Aimar reaches his limits? Nothing matters except Pingeon and his Good Samaritan, his Saint Bernard.

Abel Michéa wrote this for the *Miroir du Cyclisme*, a Communist sports paper that became every bit as nationalistic as the legion of war veterans when the subject was Poulidor. For the first time since the 1930s something like the mystique of the *équipe nationale* that had made the Tour so popular at *that* time began again to awaken in France. As a result, Anquetil discovered to his utter amazement that not just Poulidor and Pingeon, but also the modest Raymond Riotte, a stage winner and wearer of the yellow jersey for *one* day, were invited to all the criteriums while he himself was passed over by many of the organisers. Anquetil was so embittered by this flagrant injustice that he directed wild accusations at his friend Jean Stablinski, who had been road captain of the French team. The consequence was that a year later Stablinski joined Poulidor's team as a *domestique*.

Just as in 1965 Anquetil knew only one way of combating 'Poulidorism': an athletic feat. A good two months after the end of the Tour he established a new world hour record on the Vigorelli track in Milan, although it was not recognised because, as usual, he refused to submit to a doping test.

Anquetil was certainly not the only one to object to the way the press praised Poulidor to the skies. Media darlings are rarely among the most popular riders in the peloton. That was certainly true of Poulidor. Anquetil had an excellent reputation among the other cyclists. He was always ready to do his share of the work and anyone who did him a good turn could count on Anquetil to return the favour. Poulidor stood out by being stingy, which was the only way to survive in the poor French agrarian circles in which he had been raised. Moreover, he had the reputation of being a man who always sought to profit from the labour of others and who complained to the press about the most trivial matters. The latter was especially held against him, because it was a breach of the peloton's oath of secrecy, which was almost as strict as the *omertà* of the Mafia.

In Paris–Nice in 1966 the other riders decided to teach him a lesson. At the start of the last stage Poulidor was first overall. He seemed to have victory in his pocket, except that almost the entire peloton, including part of his own team, turned against him and gave Anquetil room to take a big enough lead to win the race. This was when Poulidor spoke the words into Robert Chapatte's microphone that were later often quoted to his discredit: 'What do you expect, there's nothing to be done about it. Anquetil is the boss of the peloton.'

Something like that just isn't done, and Poulidor's growing unpopularity among the riders also cost him the Tour de France that year. Poulidor seemed finally to be in a position to inflict a defeat on Anquetil, who after thirteen years as a pro was showing signs of wear and tear. But Anquetil had enough authority left to be able to promote his team-mate Lucien Aimar to the fore and, by means of an extensive combine of riders, deny victory to Poulidor.

All the same, Poulidor's bad reputation among riders did nothing to diminish his popularity with the public. Of course, many sportswriters were well aware of the real state of affairs, but they knew that the Poulidor legend, just like the Vietto legend, was too beautiful to attack. Roger Bastide and Jean-Louis Levreault of *Le Parisien Libéré* tried once to paint a realistic picture of Poulidor. This attempt caused such a wave of outrage that they got instructions from their editor-in-chief to adopt a different tone. This way Poupou could develop without hindrance into a national monument. During the years that he 'followed' the Tour – that is, he was seated in one of the cars that preceded the peloton – he always got louder cheers than any of the other French stars of yesteryear. No statue has as yet been raised to him in France, such as to the tennis stars Borotra, Cochet, Brugnon and Lacoste, but he has already given his name to a number of streets. And his name has even become an expression in the French language: 'a Poulidor' is someone who never quite makes it to the top.

Jacques Anquetil died at the end of 1987, and the story goes that on his deathbed he said to Poulidor: 'This time you're second again, Raymond!' Actually Poulidor was not even in France at the time, but such was his fame that even Anquetil's death seems to have served only to enhance the Poulidor legend.

8

Nice but Boring

The absolute high points of cycle sport have come during those periods in which, so far as the public was concerned, it rose above a pure test of strength. Races became dramatisations of daily life, with the major champions coming to personify the various currents that confronted each other in society at that moment in time. Not since the duels between Anquetil and Poulidor have situations of this kind been seen. This is not because of the personalities of the riders who have come to the fore during the past 35 years. After all, the Poulidor's case demonstrates that a champion's character does not have to square with his public image.

A much more important reason is that cycle racing as a spectator sport has undergone a true revolution since the 1960s. Anquetil and Poulidor owed their public image to the press, which ever since Paris–Rouen in 1869 had been the chief medium for following road races. At the time their rivalry reached its apex, the role of newspapers and magazines was gradually being assumed by television, which fundamentally changed the way in which the public could learn what was happening along the route. Journalists had always been able to take advantage of the general ignorance that existed about the progress of the race. The key hallmark of road races was, after all, that nobody could observe them in their entirety. The many millions who annually see the Tour de France pass by catch no more than a few glimpses. The team directors, who are supposed to be laying out the tactics of their riders, mostly drive well behind the peloton and often see only those who have dropped back because of a punctured tyre or a crash. Without the information about the race and the television images that they have been able to receive in their cars for some years now, they would be largely helpless. Even the riders themselves often have scarcely a clue as to what is happening in the race. Just like Fabrice del Dongo in Stendhal's *The Charterhouse of Parma*, they see only fragments of the battle in which they are taking part. Many a time a rider has crossed the line in jubilation only to hear later that he had not won at all.

Because it is impossible to observe the progress of a road race with one's own eyes, the media play a very different role than they do in other sports. Whoever wants to see a football- or tennis-match can sit in the stands and watch what is happening from start to finish. Whoever wants to know anything about the progress of a Tour, or a classic, is completely dependent on the media. That does not mean they are given a trustworthy or complete picture. These days, sportswriters covering major races have to drive either far ahead of, or far behind, the peloton, and they get to see the cyclists only before the start or after the finish. Even at the time when reporters still enjoyed the right to move among the riders, seated in a car or on the back of a motorcycle, they caught merely a glimpse of the development of the race and could only hope to be present by coincidence when important incidents took place. The major cycling journalists of the past made no attempt to give detailed accounts of races; they sought to do no more than meld the relatively scarce facts available to them into an exciting whole. For example, the article that the Belgian sportswriter Joris Jacobs considered the high point of his career was the page-and-a-half account of the great Alpine stage in the 1949 Tour that he based in its entirety on two short sentences which the reporter on the spot had been able to telegraph from Aosta to Belgium.

x x x

Radio reporters, too, had the freedom to interpret the course of the race in their very own way. If their equipment had not been set up in time, something that happened on occasions, they had to invent a complete account of the finish. Normally this did not become generally known, except when mistakes were made that could not be explained away. For example, the Dutch journalist Jan Cottaar was caught out in 1954 when he described the arrival at the finish of Wout Wagtmans, who in reality had quit the race. Some years later, Cottaar's compatriot, Theo Koomen, would exploit his privileged position as a reporter much more systematically: when he covered the Tour on the back of a motorcycle and was called upon to say something during the race, his listeners could always count on hearing an excited report about a barrage of breakaways, even if at that moment the riders were actually chatting with each other while pedalling along peacefully.

With the coming of television, tricks like that have become impossible. The viewers see exactly the same images as the reporters, and although the latter can naturally influence the public's views by their commentary, they are much more constrained than their colleagues of pre-TV days. That is not to say, of course, that television gives a genuinely faithful picture of the unfolding of the race, if only because it is impossible even with three or four cameras to give a complete overview of the route. Most of the time the stars and the riders at the front are the centre of attention, even though sometimes much more interesting things are happening elsewhere. Moreover, cameramen and directors have ample opportunity consciously to alter the image of the race, something that is all the more effective because television broadcasts always give the illusion that it is reality they are reproducing.

The clearest example of an intervention of that kind is the reporting of the 1979 World Championships in Valkenburg. The major obstacle in the course was the Cauberg, which had to be climbed eighteen times, and in order to save their strength most of the favourites let their team-mates assist them with hand-slings while climbing it. Whenever this was taking place the cameras focused exclusively on Jan Raas, who at the time was quarrelling with the sports editors of NOS, the Dutch radio and television news agency. Thus it was implied that Raas was the only offender, and he promptly got an official caution. Because Raas succeeded in winning the world championship that day, and seemed to have won his title unfairly, the affair stained his reputation permanently. In Italy, there was so much indignation that a few days after Raas had won the title a spectator brought him down violently during a time trial there. Raas would have been saved a lot of grief if the NOS cameras had veered away from him and focused on the Italian Francesco Moser, who climbed the Cauberg in the same way as Raas, but escaped criticism.

x x x

The most important consequence of the coming of television was that it largely ended the myth-making about cycle sport. Now that the public itself could see the races on the screen, instead of having to read overwrought descriptions of them, the riders were to a great extent divested of their legendary dimensions. Sports journalists continued to play an important part in cycle sport, because their comments, stories, and interviews helped to provide the riders who were visible on the screen with identity and personality, but it was no longer a leading part. Anquetil and Poulidor were the last real heroes in the history of cycle sport, because their rivalry unfolded just before the end of the age in which the written and spoken word mattered more than the images. To be sure, the apotheosis of their duel was the legendary television coverage of their *mano a mano* struggle on the slopes of the Puy de Dôme in the 1964 Tour, but that owed its drama above all to the press campaigns that had preceded it. If these had not taken place, the battle would certainly not 'have divided France into two' as was said at the time, and would have caused no more excitement than the duel between Laurent Fignon and Bernard Hinault in 1984. People followed the latter battle with a lot of interest and even passion, but it never transcended a purely sporting rivalry. This, despite the fact that the backgrounds of the two men provided material for a heroic duel of the old kind: Hinault was a provincial who settled down as a farmer, and Fignon was a Parisian 'intellectual' (he wears glasses and for a while pursued university studies) with long hair and a taste for frequenting discotheques.

Myth-making about cycle racing is also impeded because television has shown that the rosy-hued image presented over the decades by the print media only partially conforms to reality. As coverage extends and at times comes to include races in their entirety, it becomes increasingly clear that they can be deadly dull. This does not necessarily keep the print media from producing exciting accounts, even if the task is often not easy. Thus the early stages of the 1968 Tour were extremely uninteresting because none of the favourites, such as Poulidor, Roger Pingeon, and Jan Janssen, was willing to take the initiative. When journalists kept complaining about this in their articles, Tour director Félix Lévitan responded that what was needed was different sportswriters, not different riders. The press promptly went on strike, but Lévitan was surely not altogether wrong. A novelist and poet like Dino Buzzati knew how to turn even a totally uneventful stage into something special, but even the best TV directors cannot transform a race in which nothing happens into an exciting spectacle.

x x x

The first great champion who had to compete with the shades of his legendary predecessors under these new conditions was Eddy Merckx. As Tour winner he succeeded Jan Janssen, whose most memorable moment was still captured by radio as he sobbed to his three-year-old daughter: 'Karin, little one, Daddy has won the Tour de France.' Merckx came on the scene at a time when all the major races in France, Italy, and Belgium were being transmitted live, although they rarely appeared on television in countries like Holland. And because the public were able to see almost all his victories on TV with their own eyes, Merckx came to be surrounded by far fewer myths than the champions of an earlier generation.

As a consequence, by no means everyone is convinced that Merckx was as great a rider as Fausto Coppi, even though he scored twice as many major wins in his career as the *campionissimo*. For example, Gian Paolo Ormezzano writes in his *Storia del ciclismo* (*History of Cycling*) that Merckx was 'the strongest' but Coppi 'the greatest'. This is no simple expression of Italian chauvinism. Jacques Goddet actually went a bit further and said that Merckx was the best but Coppi was still better. According to Raphaël Géminiani, Coppi was unquestionably number one. His chief argument was that Coppi's rivals were of much higher quality than those Merckx had to face. After all, Coppi had to match himself against men like Bartali, Koblet, Kübler, Van Steenbergen and Bobet, definitely greater stars than the riders Merckx had to do battle with. But the only criterion by which Coppi's rivals can be compared with Merckx's is their reputation. And in that respect the superstars of the 1940s and 1950s, adulated by the press of the time, enjoy an enormous advantage. Even after a crushing defeat Bartali could be compared to a hero straight out of the *Iliad*. Television, on the other hand, showed so clearly how ineffectual riders like Felice Gimondi, Joop Zoetemelk and Lucien van Impe were against a Merckx in top form that even the most gifted journalists and commentators could not transform them into demigods.

Merckx's style of riding would undoubtedly have fitted much better into the era when sports fans could keep track of bicycle road racing only by means of the press. Races that can be watched on television are exciting and tense only when the potential winners are in each other's proximity. The duel between Anquetil and Poulidor on the Puy de Dôme became a TV classic because both riders were constantly in the picture together and for many minutes did not yield an inch to each other. Most legendary races from the press era were altogether different. Coppi's reputation depended in the first place on the long solo rides in which he pulled ever farther ahead of his competitors. It was these victories that led journalists to write their most epic descriptions. When Dino Buzzati covered the 1949 Giro d'Italia as a special reporter for the *Corriere della Sera*, he compared Coppi's victory over Bartali to Achilles's triumph over Hector, and larded Coppi's account of his hours-long lonely escape over the Alpine cols with citations from Homer. And yet it cannot be doubted that television coverage of this heroic stage would have been extraordinarily tedious, because the most splendid victories unfortunately often yield the most boring images. One example is Charley Mottet's triumph in the 1988 Tour of Lombardy. At the moment coverage began he was five minutes clear of his pursuers. At the end of the broadcast, more than an hour later, this lead was unchanged. Gino Bartali, who had undergone an operation but managed to get himself released from hospital early so he could be present at the finish line, for once omitted his customary sour comments. 'That's the way *we* used to win,' he noted with satisfaction. But that was exactly the problem. Long, lonely escapes are not suited to the television era.

Merckx, who had as many successful solo rides to his credit as Coppi, often felt their detrimental consequences. When he broke away 50 kilometres before the finish in the 1972 Liège–Bastogne–Liège and then gradually built up a lead of more than two-and-a-half minutes at the finish, the television journalist Marc Jeuniau told him:

> If you had been a little less impatient we would have had a marvellous broadcast: twenty kilometres farther along the TV coverage began, and at that moment your breakaway would have been much better appreciated. For three-quarters of an hour people saw only you on the screen. That is nice, but after a while it becomes boring.

Jeuniau stated right away that he just wanted to 'poke fun' at Merckx, but many a wise word is spoken in jest. Jeuniau, of course, indicated precisely why Merckx's accomplishments so often left the public cold. It was typical that his most stunning victories brought him far fewer enthusiastic letters than his half-failed 1971 Liège–Bastogne–Liège, when after a solo ride of 90 kilometres with a lead of as much as five minutes he suffered a real *défaillance*, was caught by Georges Pintens three kilometres before the finish and yet still managed to win.

Every time Coppi won a crushing victory it added a bit to his legend, while the degree to which Merckx dominated his opponents began to work *against* him over time. In the hope that the tedium of his persistent victories would be broken, the journalists eagerly seized on every sign of weakness to proclaim the end of Merckx's rule. Unfortunately, all too often this led the Belgian to yield to the temptation of making excuses for his defeats: 'At breakfast I ate grapefruit. My stomach failed to digest it.' 'All day long I felt a heavy load on my liver.' 'My left leg hurt so much that I had real difficulty pushing on the pedals.' 'I was unable to eat all day, and last night I hardly slept a wink.' 'I felt ill at the start and suffered from acid indigestion.' Very likely all of it was true – in his heyday only unusual circumstances managed to keep Merckx from victory – but it made a bad fit with the sort of heroism that was ascribed to the champions of the past. Even Hector's image would have suffered irreparable damage if he had blamed his defeat by Achilles on acid indigestion. Bartali understood better what was expected from him. In the 1949 Giro, when two flat tyres contributed to his defeat by Coppi in the Dolomites, a fan asked him the next day: 'Did you have two or three punctures yesterday?' Bartali's answer was sublime: 'Punctures? We never get punctures.'

x x x

Although Merckx did not always tend his public relations as carefully as he should have, it is certain that there has never been another rider quite like him. He won more than anybody else, could always be found at the front, and was under all circumstances ready to attack. Moreover, he was dangerous on every kind of terrain. At the time he signed his first professional contract, dominion over the world of cycling was split between two great champions. Anquetil ruled the major stage-races and Rik van Looy the classics. Neither made much of an effort to expand his domain at the other's expense. Merckx was everywhere, however, from the Omloop Het Volk in the early spring to the Tour of Lombardy in the autumn, and he always tried to win. Even in the major Tours he often left few crumbs for others. When he made his debut in the 1969 Tour, he won six stages, the yellow and green jerseys, the mountain prize and the combined classification. On this occasion the French cyclist Christian Raymond gave him a nickname so apt that it promptly gained general acceptance: 'the cannibal.'

Merckx's 'cannibalism' unquestionably matched his temperament to the full. But it was also a consequence of the structure of cycle racing in his era. To maintain his market value in the Belgian criteriums and track races, Merckx had to do well in the races that traditionally yielded the greatest prestige in his country: the Tour de France, the classics in his own country and in northern France. Although this constituted an extensive programme, he could not limit himself to it. In his heyday he rode for Italian companies, the only sponsors who, because of the high cost of TV commercials in their country, were ready to spend enough money on their cycling teams to be able to afford a champion of Merckx's calibre. That meant, of course, that he was expected to show up for the Giro, Milan–San Remo, the Tour of Lombardy, and a number of lesser Italian races – and to win them if possible. This way he had a considerably fuller agenda than his predecessors. In the years before the First World War, Henri Pélissier and Lucien Petit-Breton participated in roughly 30 races a season; after 1945, Coppi and Bartali took part in 60 to 80. Merckx and his successors appeared at the start line more than 150 times a year.

Merckx was so strong that his sway could only have been broken by a united coalition of his competitors. In principle there were ample grounds for forming such a coalition, because he claimed so many major victories, and the publicity that came with them, that potential sponsors hesitated to invest money in racing teams if they were unable to get Merckx. Moreover, more than once a criterium was cancelled because the organisers had not succeeded in engaging the 'cannibal'. As usual, there was so much rivalry between the riders that joint action rarely came about. Those who sought to attack Merckx's supremacy could count at most on the benevolent neutrality of the peloton, so most such attempts suffered shipwreck. Besides, the cyclists who dared to make the attempt had to extend themselves so much that it seriously shortened their careers. Luis Ocaña, José Manuel Fuente, Bernard Thévénet and Cyrille Guimard are really the only ones who tried to do battle with Merckx on equal terms, and it is surely no coincidence that none of them stayed at the top for long. When Guimard took up the fight with Merckx during the 1972 Tour he was not even able to complete the race. In spite of daily injections of novocaine in his knees, he had to quit the field a few days before the end, and he was not yet 30 when he ended his racing career.

No wonder most riders acquiesced in the inevitable and resigned themselves to Merckx's rule, especially because, after his tempestuous beginning, he was increasingly willing to leave the consolation prizes for others. He arranged for his compatriots Walter Godefroot and Patrick Sercu to become points winners in the Tours of 1970 and 1974, because the green jersey would have added nothing to his lustre anyway. He was even willing to give Felice Gimondi the opportunity to restore his damaged reputation with a win in Ghent-Wevelgem, and it was not his fault that Roger Swerts spoiled the Italian's plans. Rik van Looy initially tried to resist his countryman's advance with all his might, but he was in the closing stages of his career, and in the 1969 Tour he actually had to make a deal with Merckx in order to win one stage. Roger De Vlaeminck, who presented himself in 1970 and 1971 as the 'anti-Merckx', abandoned his systematic opposition thereafter and was satisfied with one or two classics annually. Joop Zoetemelk, Lucien van Impe and many others generally preferred to undertake no initiatives of their own in the hope that Merckx would slip up now and then. Other strong riders, such as the Belgian Herman van Springel and the Dutchman Rini Wagtmans, abandoned their personal ambitions altogether and entered the service of the 'cannibal', who as a result had at his disposal a team every bit as strong as those that had once served Van Looy and Anquetil.

Just like Anquetil, Merckx became the boss of the peloton. Riders who wanted to chance their arm and go for one of the easier stages in the Tour or Giro had to ask his permission first. The only other rider in this period who commanded anything like a similar authority was Felice Gimondi, but he very quickly acknowledged Merckx's supremacy and functioned at most as a kind of viceroy.

Merckx's authority was so great that he sometimes acted as a sort of supervisor in order to maintain law and order in the peloton. He exhibited the most telling exercise of this role during the 1976 Tour of Romandie. Roger De Vlaeminck had decided he wanted to win this stage-race, and in order to force Merckx's team to make an extra effort (Merckx on this occasion was a rival rather than an ally), he sent his trusted *domestique* Johan de Muynck ahead with a small group. De Muynck was not brought back and captured the leader's jersey. Two days later, he and De Vlaeminck succeeded in escaping from Merckx. The expectation, of course, was that De Muynck, who was already 28 and had never given any sign of personal ambition, would fall back discreetly, allowing his team's leader to win the race in fine fashion. Instead he broke away and finished first, much to De Vlaeminck's rage. The peloton's *domestiques*, who are mostly Coppi wannabes, loved it, and jokes about Johan de Vlaemuynck were everywhere. The top riders were less amused, because if *domestiques* can rebel successfully, the whole hierarchical structure of the cycling world and with it the position of the leaders is under threat. According to unwritten laws a *domestique* may ride for his own interest only when for one reason or another his team's top rider is no longer able to win. Sometimes many years can pass before an opportunity like this presents itself, as in the case of Pino Cerami, who gained the first of his three victories in classics only after he had turned 38. Yet genuine attempts at rebellion are rarely undertaken and usually they are punished severely. A famous example is the case of Benoni Beheyt, who in 1963 managed to snaffle the world championship from his team leader Van Looy. From that moment on, the 'Emperor of Herentals' used the enormous influence he had over the peloton and with the organisers of criteriums to thwart his disobedient team-mate in every possible way. Three years later Beheyt, who was still only 26, realised he no longer had a future as a professional racing cyclist and ended his career.

De Vlaeminck did not have as much authority as Van Looy, and he was therefore forced to call on Merckx for help while the Tour of Romandie was still in progress. One day earlier the two had still been fierce rivals, but now that a higher principle was at issue they joined forces to call De Muynck to order. During the morning stage on the last day Merckx broke away first. De Muynck caught him, and both riders dropped back to the peloton. At that moment De Vlaeminck broke away, so that De Muynck was forced into renewed exertion. Then it was Merckx's turn again. And so it went, right to the end of the stage. The goal was to exhaust De Muynck so that he would be too fatigued to give a good account of himself in the time trial that afternoon. But Merckx and De Vlaeminck evidently tired themselves more than De Muynck, who won the time trial and with it the Tour of Romandie.

If it had been De Vlaeminck's call, De Muynck would certainly have lost his place on the team because of his rebellious attitude. The team's director, Franco Cribiori, took a different view, however. De Vlaeminck was a major force in one-day races, but he was never quite good enough as a climber to win a major stage-race. And two weeks after the Tour of Romandie, the Giro d'Italia would begin, the most important race of the season for the Brooklyn chewing gum company, the Italian sponsor of both De Muynck and De Vlaeminck. Now that Cribiori suddenly had a potential candidate for victory available to him, he did not want to drop him just like that. On his insistence the two riders made a pact, undertaking to support each other so that one of them would win the Giro. De Muynck enjoyed his best form ever and succeeded in capturing the pink leader's jersey three days before the end. De Vlaeminck had no intention of helping his rebellious *domestique* gain the victory, and, together with his lieutenant, Roland De Witte, dropped out. It is not known exactly what then happened behind the scenes, but in the concluding time trial, when De Muynck appeared at the start line, there was no one from his team with an escort car to support him with a spare bike in case of breakdown, or to keep him informed about the time differences among the riders.

It would have been splendid, of course, if De Muynck had won in spite of this. But not all cycling races unfold like a boys' adventure book. He lost the pink jersey to Felice Gimondi by nineteen seconds. The happy end did not come until two years later, when De Muynck had left De Vlaeminck's team to join Gimondi's and was able to capitalise on his second opportunity to win the Giro.

x x x

De Muynck was an outstanding rider but no superman, and his rebellion in the Tour of Romandie succeeded only because Merckx's rule was nearing its end. That spring Merckx had gained the last major victory of his career in the 1976 Milan–San Remo, and the battle to succeed him had already begun. The chief candidate was his compatriot Freddy Maertens, who won 54 races that year, among them eight stages of the Tour de France (in which he finished eighth) and the world championship.

At any other moment in cycling history, a Belgian with that kind of success would at once have become a national hero. Alas,

Maertens was unfortunate in that his rise occurred when Merckx was still lord and master. In Belgium the 'cannibal' was revered like a god, if only because in 1969 he had finally given his country the Tour victory it had awaited for 30 long years. There was really no room for any other stars. When Roger De Vlaeminck won the 1969 national championship in his rookie year, he was treated to a chorus of whistles, not because there was anything to criticise about his riding but because he had assumed the place the public had reserved for Merckx.

Freddy Maertens, too, continually had to contend with Merckx's shadow. Even after the 80 victories he gained in his first three years as a professional, he still was not really popular because he had publicly held Merckx responsible for his defeat in the 1973 World Championship. It is true that Merckx's glory days were past, but he still had great appeal to the public, if only because he had set a standard against which the qualities of every potential champion could be measured. To capture his own deserved place in the sun, Maertens was therefore obliged to behave just as cannibalistically as Merckx. And that he was capable of doing so he proved in the 1977 Tour of Spain, in which he not only won overall victory, and the points classification, but thirteen of the nineteen stages as well. In that year's Giro, too, he won seven stages before he was forced out with a broken wrist.

Maertens won most of his victories in time trials and in end-of-stage sprints, in which he was almost unbeatable. To show himself the equal of Merckx, though, he had to demonstrate that he was also capable of impressive solo rides. In the Flèche Wallonne of 1977 he was head and shoulders above the competition and could easily have bided his time until the final sprint. Instead, he broke away 45 kilometres from the finish in order to arrive there with a three-minute lead.

In spite of his broken wrist Maertens tallied 53 victories in 1977, and even Eddy Merckx had to admit he was the strongest rider in the peloton. But from that moment on his results declined swiftly. In 1978 he won only eighteen races, and when he was able to take only a couple of kermesses during the next two years, his career seemed to have reached a definitive end, even though he was only twenty-eight. Maertens was one of the first to make frequent use of the 12-tooth sprocket, and his fall was generally ascribed to the destructive toll that the use of this gear, once thought to be super-high, had taken on his body. What argued against this was that he was never bothered by tendinitis in his knees or Achilles tendons – the evil that almost inevitably afflicts riders who push themselves too hard. The hypothesis that Maertens was physically quite worn out was completely controverted in 1981 when, to the astonishment of all experts, he suddenly won five stages in the Tour as well as the points classification, and on top of that became world champion in the autumn.

Maertens was certainly not the first rider to demonstrate that he had been mistakenly written off, but his comeback was so surprising that there seemed to be no rational explanation for it. No wonder that all kinds of wild rumours were soon doing the rounds. The most popular version was that Maertens was using drugs that could not yet be detected by the doping tests. Envious colleagues fed this rumour by saying that his urine was poison green and that during the race he careened through the peloton like a drunkard.

True, with respect to doping Maertens certainly did not have a squeaky clean past (no more so than Merckx, Gimondi, Zoetemelk, Thévénet and many others), but if indeed some kind of miracle pills existed, it is hardly credible that he alone would have known of them. It cannot be supposed that the pharmacists in his home town of Lombardsijde were that much better than those in the rest of Europe.

He himself has always presented his decline and recovery as a mental matter. Since the publication of his autobiography, *Niet van horen zeggen* (*Not from Hearsay*), this explanation seems a lot less unlikely than people assumed at the time. The main theme of his book is the systematic opposition he constantly experienced from all sides, the plots that were hatched against him, and the many times he was 'stitched up'. He even relates how at a certain point he underwent treatment by exorcists because he was (and is) convinced that certain persons, motivated by envy, had 'put a spell' on him.

This seems rather exaggerated, but no one need doubt that Maertens was constantly hindered in his career, and that he had to struggle against a fair number of coalitions and combines. And it is obvious that the peloton was not prepared to support Maertens in his efforts to become a second Merckx. *One* cannibal in a generation is more than enough. Yet the opposition Maertens experienced did not differ in principle from the gauntlet every new talent has to run. At the outset of his career Eddy Merckx was not treated in a very friendly fashion either, but he was mentally better equipped to deal with it than Maertens. Except when a spectator gave him a blow while he was on Puy de Dôme during the 1975 Tour, Merckx never gave any sign that either the public or his colleagues had disturbed his equilibrium. Maertens was psychologically much more vulnerable, and when he also weakened physically after his wrist fracture in 1977, he became easy prey for the 'mafia' in the peloton, as he himself referred to it. In this he was surely neither the first nor the last. A bicycle race is governed by a constant conflict of interests. No gifts are given, and whoever wants to maintain himself at the top needs to be mentally very strong. It is no accident, after all, that many talented riders prefer the safe role of *domestique*.

Character

The Circuit de Châteaulin in Brittany ranks as the most important criterium in France. The appearance fees are high, and every year the organisers manage to attract the strongest riders of the day. The honour roll contains as many big names as that of Milan–San Remo or Paris–Roubaix: Bobet, Van Steenbergen, Van Looy, Anquetil, Poulidor, De Vlaeminck, Ocaña, Merckx, Moser, Zoetemelk, Hinault, Fignon, Miguel Induráin, Laurent Jalabert, and Marco Pantani. But in spite of the prestige it enjoyed, Circuit proceeds just like any other criterium. This means that some local shopkeeper who offers a prize has the right to choose its winner, but the distribution of the other prizes is decided by a coalition of star cyclists, who take the lion's share for themselves and give the rest to their *domestiques* and the occasional outsider.

Usually this arrangement works out without problems, but not in 1975. Each time the designated rider got himself ready to win an intermediate sprint prize by a tyre's width, a young, unknown Breton attacked fiercely and threatened to throw a spanner into the works. Of course he was unable to withstand the supremacy of the ruling coalition, although he did compel the stars to greater exertions than they had counted on. It goes without saying that they did not appreciate this, especially because the criterium tour was already an exhausting business due to the constant travel back and forth (although the results were unimportant, more amphetamines were taken than in all the rest of the year). The Breton ignored the rain of curses he had to endure. Finally Merckx cut the Gordian knot: he pulled up alongside the rebel and told him he could share in the prizes provided he kept a low profile. That was how Bernard Hinault joined the cycling elite.

Hinault proved in Châteaulin that he possessed the character of a future star; in 1977 he demonstrated that he also had the necessary athletic qualities. That season he won two classics and the Grand Prix des Nations. Moreover, during the important Dauphiné Libéré stage-race he provided French television with the most sensational sports transmission of the year. During the descent of the Col de Porte, before the eyes of millions of viewers, he disappeared into a ravine, reappeared moments later with a bleeding head, grabbed a backup bike without hesitating for an instant, and rode on to win the stage.

In 1978 Merckx and Gimondi said their farewells, and during his debut in the Tour that year Hinault demonstrated beyond the shadow of a doubt that he was their rightful successor, not only by arriving in Paris wearing the yellow jersey, but also by exacting from the other riders the respect that is awarded only to a *patron*, a boss. The occasion for this came during an apparently unimportant 'transitional stage' from Tarbes to Valence d'Agen. The day before, the peloton had been forced to ride one of the toughest stages of the Tour, with three first-category cols. After the finish the riders were put on buses which took two hours to reach the starting point of the next stage. Only after this could they be massaged and begin their dinner; they didn't get to bed until midnight. The next morning they had to get up at five because there were two half-stages on the agenda that day, requiring an unusually early start. Furthermore, that evening they would have to travel another 150 kilometres by bus. No wonder the riders were in an extremely bad mood that day. To make their displeasure known, they maintained a very slow tempo. That was the traditional form of protest, but this time the cyclists decided they needed to take stronger measures.

When, after many hours, they reached Valence d'Agen, the whole peloton got off their bikes and just stood there instead of crossing the finish line. With the exception of the well-behaved Joop Zoetemelk, all of the top riders were to be found at the front. The man who spoke on behalf of the peloton was not André Chalmel, chairman of the union of French professional bicycle racers, or Freddy Maertens, the rider with the most illustrious list of achievements, but the rookie Bernard Hinault. This was all the more remarkable because his team director, Cyrille Guimard, was at that moment involved in a serious conflict with the agents Roger Piel and Daniel Dousset, who represented most of the French professionals.

Hinault did not succeed in arousing much sympathy for the riders' action. The public felt they had been cheated, and the organisers were furious. The mayor of Valence d'Agen, the politician Baylet, who had dreamed of appearing on TV in the living rooms of millions of homes side by side with the wearer of the yellow jersey, reacted with a flood of abuse to Hinault's offer to come and ride a criterium gratis after the end of the Tour. Most journalists were at least as negative in their comments the next day. The heroic image of the sport, already seriously tarnished, was completely shattered now that the 'giants of the road' had gone on strike because they were not allowed to get a good night's sleep. The old hands especially pointed out that the Tour had been a lot tougher in the past: in the 1930s the starting signal had often been given as early as four in the morning and occasionally three stages had been completed in one day. But since that time the riders' outlook had changed. They were better-educated, more articulate, and more self-confident than their predecessors. Especially in the Netherlands, where the wave of democratisation had raged more violently in the 1970s than elsewhere, a generation of riders of a wholly new type had emerged. Most of them were united in the Ti-Raleigh team which, by analogy to the total football of the mighty Ajax team of the 1970s, introduced a sort of total bike racing without a strict hierarchy, in which *domestiques* and top riders could take each others' places at any given moment. It was certainly no coincidence, then, that four of the eight cyclists who stood in the first row in Valence d'Agen came from this team: Hennie Kuiper, Gerben Karstens, Gerrie Knetemann, and Jan Raas. The last-mentioned did not, in contrast with the others, suffer the howling and whistling of the crowd with a grim face, but stood there calmly, reading a newspaper.

The riders' strike in Valence d'Agen had some initial success: one of the next stages was shortened, and in 1979 the course of the Tour included far fewer transfers between the finish of one stage and the start of the next than the year before. But in 1980 the number of transfers increased once again, although this time the organisers took greater account of the riders' need for sleep than in 1978. In 1982, in fact, a new record was established: only nine times out of twenty-two did the start take place in the same town where the previous day's stage had ended. Of course, the Tour directors thereby ran the risk of renewed industrial action by the riders, but they had no choice. Financing the Tour was a huge, recurring problem. The developments that first became noticeable at the end of the 1930s continued. The additional sales of the organising papers made but a small contribution to meeting the total costs. *Le Parisien Libéré*, which was not exclusively a sports paper, drew scarcely any profit from its organising role, while *L'Equipe*'s daily circulation, which averaged roughly 300,000, increased by only 100,000 during the Tour. The bulk of the 10 million francs (rather more than a million pounds) that the Tour's organisation cost by the end of the 1970s had to come from other sources. The amounts that towns were prepared to pay for the privilege of hosting the start or finish of a stage played a key part in this. Fortunately, since the introduction of TV coverage, many tourist resorts were eager to pay a hefty sum of money to host the Tour. This was especially true of the newly-built ski-resorts, where the hotels were generally half empty in summer. Often they were located on a mountain peak, which usually provided an extremely exciting television spectacle and led to a large number of viewers.

All the same, such a happy combination of sporting and commercial interests was, from the point of view of the Tour's directors, really quite unnecessary. When the market gardeners and vegetable exporters of Brittany came up with 1,800,000 francs (around £200,000) in 1974, in return they got a prologue, two stages, plus a stage in England that was introduced for the sole purpose of giving publicity to the launching of a ferry service between Roscoff and Plymouth. Because of the boat trip there and the flight back, the riders were so fatigued that not only the stages in Brittany but also the ones that followed were totally uninteresting from a sporting point of view. In 1981, when three Belgian cities were willing to come up with a large amount of money, and nowhere between Brussels and southern Alsace was there a town that had made a higher bid, the riders had to complete three stages in Belgium and then take the plane to Mulhouse. The exception to this was the Planckaert brothers, Eddy and Walter, who feared flying and therefore had to travel more than six hours by car. The directors of other races were also constantly on the lookout for the most lucrative, not the most attractive route. From the moment when Milan offered more money than Como to host the finish, the Tour of Lombardy followed a route that for years made a boring finish all but inevitable.

Cities that were willing to finance the finish or start of a stage were not the only source of income for the Tour. All the teams had to pay a substantial registration fee. The number prepared to meet this condition gradually declined over the years, the low point being reached in 1977 when only ten showed up at the start. The most important financial contribution, of course, came from the sponsors.

They paid for a place in the advertising caravan and for the right to put their company name everywhere possible: cars, banners, flags, billboards, canteens, cyclist's numbers, jerseys, caps, socks, shoes, bouquets of flowers and every other object that might show up on the TV screen. In the 1960s and 1970s these payments were not large. Very few businesses were prepared to spend big money, and the Tour directors had to exert themselves each year to rustle up enough cash. That was also the reason why the organisers took very good care that every penny paid for advertising went into their own coffers. In 1978 in the Groenoordhallen in Leiden, where the Tour prologue would begin that year, Félix Lévitan saw advertising signs for companies that had paid money to the local organisers but not to the Tour management. Immediately he ruled that the prologue must be 'neutralised': the riders had to complete the course but their times would not be calculated into the general standings. Lévitan had the good fortune that it had rained that day, so that he could unexpectedly translate his decision into sporting terms: the roads would be too dangerous to ride at full speed. It did not sound very credible. After all, the race was sent into the mountains of the Alps and Pyrenees in mist and thunderstorms. But all protests were in vain. The result was that the winner of the prologue, Jan Raas, was furious to learn that he would not get the yellow jersey. When a champion becomes really annoyed, it can spur him to great things: the next day in Sint-Willebrord, Raas was victorious again and officially took first place in the general classification. To complete his revenge he then refused the yellow jersey offered to him, a gesture that would have pleased Henri Pélissier.

The incident in Leiden is perhaps the only case in which the inscriptions on advertising hoardings exercised an influence on the course of the race. It is quite different with the sponsorship of the many special classifications that have been incorporated into the Tour, and other major tours. In the Tour this began in modest fashion with a mountain prize that was offered for the first time in 1908 by the Labor and Hutchinson companies, and has been a fixed part of the Tour since 1933. A team classification was added later, and since 1953 a points classification, as well. It didn't end there. The fantasy of the sponsors was so inexhaustible that the Tour was enriched with classifications for the best young riders, sprints within stages, team points, combination of rankings, attendance, and with prizes for the rider who has made the greatest advance in the classifications, the best team-mate, the most lovable, most unfortunate, friendliest, most elegant rider et cetera. Most of these prizes had hardly any sporting value, but they were coveted all the same because they yielded money and publicity. This applied especially to the classifications that led to a podium tribute at the end of each stage.

Directors and television cameramen did get instructions from on high that the filming of company names was permitted only when these were a part of the 'action' taking place at that moment. The concept of 'action' is vague, of course, and the Tour management and television editors were prepared to interpret it as liberally as possible. A firm that looked after the sponsorship of some special classification could safely expect that TV directors would hold the presentation of one of the appropriate jerseys to be 'action'. As a result the coverage of every finish was concluded with lengthy tributes to various riders, most of whom had no idea of how to behave in front of the camera. Images of this kind not only made the conclusions of Tour TV broadcasts well-nigh unbearable, but indirectly had a negative effect on the liveliness of the race as well. In the light of the attention paid to them by television, the publicity value of the special classifications was substantial, so there were always teams that had something to defend and therefore some benefit in ensuring that as little as possible happened in the race.

It is self-evident that these developments, however necessary they were for the continued existence of the Tour, were not greeted with general enthusiasm. After the riders reached the Champs Elysées during the last stage in 1981, the new socialist Minister of Sports, Edwige Avice, followed the peloton in Jacques Goddet's car. Afterwards she stated that she was 'shocked' by the aggressively commercial character of the Tour. According to her the peloton was little more than a 'second advertising caravan'. She was particularly annoyed by the many logos that yellow-jersey wearer Bernard Hinault wore on his clothing and his bicycle. The minister had not counted them, but in fact there were 22 from seven different companies. That was half again as many as Merckx had worn ten years before and three times the number of logos visible on Anquetil's bike and clothing 20 years earlier.

Félix Lévitan, the financial brain behind the Tour, accepted the minister's critique, only to ignore it. After all, he couldn't do much about it. To augment the precarious budget of his Tour he needed every franc. Only when sponsors were willing to pay millions for their presence in the Tour could the directors afford to abolish all these fantasy classifications. That is not to say that Lévitan did not look for other solutions. Because of the way he was able to pry the last franc out of potential sponsors and other financiers, he was often made out to be nothing more than a money-grubber. And yet there was a lot more to him than that. Few other people have contributed so much to the development of cycle sport since the war. Moreover, in the flourishing 1950s Lévitan was probably the first to worry about the future of the Tour de France. Although, even then, it ranked among the great sporting events in the world, its base was very small, certainly compared with that of the Olympic Games and the football World Cup. In fact, professional bicycle road racing was limited at the time to a small part of Western Europe: France, Italy, Belgium, Spain, the Netherlands, Switzerland, and Luxembourg.

Lévitan did not want to acquiesce in this state of affairs. At a very early stage he was playing with the idea of opening the Tour to amateurs. He knew, of course, that this was unrealisable in the short term, and therefore as an intermediate phase he created a stage-race in 1961 that took place during the Tour and followed the part of the same route: the Tour de l'Avenir. Already in the first year he managed to attract riders from countries that until then had never been represented in the Tour, such as Sweden, Norway, Finland, and Uruguay. After six editions, Lévitan thought the transition period had lasted long enough, and at the end of 1966 he announced that the next Tour would be open to all categories. This met with so much resistance – the Union of French Professional Racing Cyclists, led by Anquetil, even threatened a boycott – that the Tour management had to drop the plan for the time being.

In his efforts to transform the Tour into a global event, Lévitan was hardly driven by idealistic motives alone. Above all, he saw it as a means of arousing more interest on the part of multinational sponsors. It therefore goes without saying that Lévitan paid a lot of attention to two countries that set the pace in economic matters in the West: the United States and Japan. It was a huge personal success for him when in 1978 an American team took part in the Tour de l'Avenir for the first time. The Japanese took longer to show up, because in their country bicycle racing is monopolised by specialists in *Keirin*, a form of track racing whose greatest attraction is that it permits heavy betting. Yet in 1983 a team of Japanese riders also appeared at the start, and two of them, Matsuyoshi Takahashi and

Yukiharu Mori, who were coddled like babies by the organisers, actually succeeded, against all expectations, in reaching the finish line.

Because in many countries women were riding at a higher level by international standards than men, Lévitan also created a *Tour Féminin* in 1984, in which teams from the United States, England, Canada, and the Netherlands, as well as two from France, took part. He had also hoped to attract a team from China – the biggest bicycle manufacturer in the world – but that did not happen until 1985. Of course this initiative, too, was far from disinterested, but that does not alter the fact that women's bicycle racing was hugely stimulated now that it could profit from the prestige of the Tour de France. The winners of the yellow and green jerseys, the American Marianne Martin and the Netherlander Mieke Havik, stood on the podium that had been erected on the Champs Elysées for Fignon, Hinault and Greg LeMond and in this way got far more publicity than had ever come the way of their predecessors.

x x x

Lévitan's plans for 'open' races were taken up in the 1970s by the managers of smaller stage-races, who hoped thereby to make their races more interesting. The first to admit amateurs to his race was Jean Leulliot, a former journalist with *L'Auto* and the organiser of Paris–Nice. In the first year, 1974, they did not have much success. The amateurs met with systematic opposition from the professionals who regarded the new initiative as an attempt to take bread out of their mouths. If one of these newcomers managed to get into a breakaway group, for example, the professionals who were part of it immediately refused to keep the escape going, so that the peloton could easily catch up. Only in the time trials were the professionals powerless to frustrate the amateurs, and it is therefore no coincidence that the latter scored their best results in these stages. In view of the experiences in Paris–Nice, not surprisingly most of the cycling federations showed little enthusiasm for exposing their riders to the Tour de France. Not until 1983 did Lévitan succeed in getting a team of amateurs to the start line. They came from Colombia, a country where cycle racing had for many years been unbelievably popular. The absence of a bicycle industry that could afford to put riders under contract in exchange for a secure salary meant that professionalism was late developing, but the prizes available to amateurs were so high that the 1948 Olympic champion, José Beyaert ('the Frenchman' in García Márquez's short stories about bicycle racing), who after a failed professional career in France had signed up for a few races in Columbia, decided to settle there permanently. Since most of the major cities, such as Bogotá, Medellin, and Calí, are located high in the mountains, Colombian races involve a lot of climbing over cols that seem to go on forever (the Paso de las Minas between Calí and Medellin rises for 45 kilometres). The roads over the passes had been constructed primarily for freight transport and so were not very steep, nor did they include hairpin bends. To become a great racing cyclist in Colombia you had to be a formidable climber; virtuosity in the valleys was not required and neither was great stamina, because the races were rarely longer than 160 kilometres.

The Colombians who took part in the Tour were therefore very different from their European colleagues. The collision between these two cycling cultures led the Colombians to ride helplessly at the rear of the peloton in the flat stages, often losing contact when the tempo increased near the finish. But in the stage over the four classic cols in the Pyrenees they demonstrated that they really *did* have to be taken into account. The established European climbers, Zoetemelk and Van Impe, were in the habit of postponing their attacks as long as possible; the Colombians Jiménez and Corredor began a furious attack during the ascent of the first col, as a result of which the stage proceeded very differently from the way it would have otherwise. Near the end of the 200-kilometre long ride the Colombians began to weaken, but through their action they had paved the way for a new generation of cyclists who broke through in this stage: Robert Millar, Pedro Delgado, Pascal Simon, and Laurent Fignon.

In 1984 the Colombians launched their super-climber Lucho Herrera, who won the short stage up to Alpe d'Huez that year. Many regarded him as a potential Tour winner, and Herrera did his best to adapt himself to the European style of bicycle racing and become a complete rider. Just as in the case of René Vietto, however, his improvements in the flat stages and time trials came at the expense of his climbing capacities.

x x x

The participation of the Colombians meant an enrichment of professional racing and provided the Tour with an important financier as well: Café de Colombia, which sponsored not only a cycling team but also the mountain prize. Still, Félix Lévitan continued to make efforts to get an American team to enter his Tour. He succeeded in 1986 when the 7-Eleven team entered for the first time. Just like the Colombians, the Americans showed they had a culture of their own, even though in a completely different way: to the great dismay of the peloton, they used the services of a masseuse. The world of European professional cyclists was certainly at that time a purely macho community, in which feminine elements, seen as threatening, were for the most part strictly taboo. This is why the atavistic superstition that sex and high performance in sport did not go together was so widespread among bike riders. It is also typical that this applied only to a limited extent to the 'groupies' along the route, who could be taken as the 'spoils of war'.

The members of the 7-Eleven team were not the first Americans to take part in the Tour. Before their arrival, the combined hunt by sponsors and organisers for American riders, which promised so much economically, had already had ample results. In 1979 the world championship for juniors was won in very convincing fashion by a certain Greg LeMond. Because bicycle racing was such a small affair in the United States, he went to France that same year to prepare for a possible career as a professional. From the very outset talent scouts watched him like hawks, and in 1980 the sports director for the Renault team, Cyrille Guimard, travelled to Nevada with his top rider, Bernard Hinault, to offer LeMond a contract. In 1982 the American won the Tour de l'Avenir in spite of the participation of strong Russian and East German teams, and a Colombian team which included Lucho Herrera. From that moment on it was clear that he was a potential Tour winner.

LeMond was not the only American professional in the peloton. His compatriot Jonathan Boyer had also turned professional in 1980, although he attracted much less interest. Boyer was a good rider, but no one thought him capable of a really big win. And yet, during the 1982 world championship at Goodwood, he seemed to be on the verge of becoming a star. Near the finish he took a lead of a few dozen metres. The timing was ideal: the finish was so close that anyone who started to chase would pull the entire bunch along and throw away his own chance of the title. Suddenly Greg LeMond sprinted with all his might towards his compatriot, to the great delight of the Italian Giuseppe Saronni, who clung to LeMond's wheel and so was ideally positioned to finish many lengths clear of everyone else. This did not trouble LeMond. Of course, he would rather have become world champion himself, but the most important thing was that he had prevented a personal catastrophe. Cycle racing was still so underdeveloped in the United States that there was room for *one* star, at most. LeMond knew he had the qualities that would enable him to claim that position, but now Boyer threatened to wreck his fine prospects. Were Boyer to become world champion, *he* would be the one to whom American sponsors would give all their attention. That, of course, had to be prevented at all costs. Boyer happened to belong to the same team as LeMond, but that could not be helped. To journalists who asked him why he had challenged his own team-mate, he said:

> I didn't think he could win, nor did I want him to win. He's just no friend of mine. I didn't think anyone like him should become world champion. Boyer knew from the start that we weren't friends and that we were both riding for ourselves. I wore the American jersey, but there really wasn't an American team and I certainly didn't belong to one. I paid for my trip to England, my hotel bills, and everything myself. If I was riding for a team it was Renault.

Riders who stitch up their own team-mates are usually looked at askance, but LeMond knew he didn't have to worry about that in this case. Boyer had very few friends in the peloton. He was a health fanatic and because, being American, he did not know the etiquette among European riders, he had in interviews more than once expressed disgust about their doping practices. He was not forgiven for this, and because someone who behaves so scandalously is thought to be capable of anything, Boyer was generally suspected of the blackest misdeeds. When Pascal Simon broke his shoulder blade in a fall in the 1983 Tour and thereby forfeited a good chance of victory, many cyclists believed Boyer to be somehow responsible. Nobody thought ill of LeMond for depriving his compatriot of the world championship – or for winning it himself a year later. From that moment on it was clear that no rider had such commercial worth as LeMond. Renault raised his salary to $100,000 annually, twice as much as Tour winner Laurent Fignon. All the same, it was inevitable that he would sooner or later enter the service of another company, because Renault had comparatively little interest in the US market. True, during the 1984 Tour LeMond assured everybody that he had no intention of changing teams, but straight after its conclusion he opened negotiations with Bernard Tapie, the managing director of La Vie Claire, Look, Mic-Mac and a host of other firms. Tapie had earned a fortune buying bankrupt companies, which he transformed into profitable enterprises through a change of management and new investment. He applied the same formula to cycle racing. In 1984 he built a team around Bernard Hinault, who had undergone a major knee operation and whom the surgeons gave only a 50-50 chance of regaining his old level. This time, too, Tapie showed good business instincts. Hinault did not manage to win the Tour, but his aggressive style of riding made him more popular than ever. As a result, just from the sale of Mic-Mac's shirts, their design inspired by one of Mondrian's paintings, Tapie more than recovered his investment. This was despite the fact that initially they had been the laughing-stock of the peloton.

Tapie directed his commercial activities mostly towards France at first. Then, when annual sales of his empire were approaching the equivalent of £250 million in 1984, he thought the time had come to explore new markets, specifically in the United States. With an eye to this he wanted to get LeMond under contract at any price. This was not very hard: he simply offered him a base salary of $1 million for three years, more than tripling the amount Renault was willing to pay. In this way, LeMond became by far the best-paid cyclist in the world. Tapie made no secret of the fact that Greg owed this privileged position above all to his nationality. 'If he hadn't been an American,' Tapie said, 'it would have been a zero less.' (Later he would claim he was merely referring to the negotiating skills of LeMond's father, but that was only after it became clear that his foray into America had been unsuccessful.) To give his team as international a character as possible, Tapie contracted, besides LeMond, Hinault and several other French riders and a second American, Andy Hampsten, the Swiss cyclists Niki Rüttimann and Guido Winterberg, the Canadian Steve Bauer, and the Dane Kim Andersen.

In the Tour of 1985 Hinault started as the top rider of the La Vie Claire team, with LeMond as his lieutenant. Since Hinault's fantastic *palmarès* meant that he occupied a higher place in the cycling hierarchy than his team-mate, this was the only possible division of roles. Bernard Tapie had to acquiesce in this, even if in his heart of hearts he hoped for a victory by his American star – far more interesting from a publicity point of view. Assistant team director Maurice Le Guilloux said later that Tapie was unable to resist constantly spurring LeMond on to the offensive. When the American responded in the Pyrenees, and seemed to have a realistic chance of winning the Tour, Tapie, who could not afford conflict with the popular Hinault, gave him instructions to hold back. LeMond hardly understood this and felt cheated, but he did obey and rode on in faithful service to his team leader, who arrived in Paris as the winner.

As Tapie saw it, Hinault had now received his due, and because business is business, after all, the next year he would have to make way for his American team-mate. Hinault, knowing how difficult his fifth Tour victory had been, agreed. Upon his arrival in Paris he solemnly promised that the next year he would do everything possible to help the American to victory.

As promised, LeMond started as the leader of the La Vie Claire team in the 1986 Tour, with Hinault cast in the sympathetic role of the star who helps his young team-mate to the victory. In their time, Bartali and Poulidor had earned enormous popularity in this role, but they were able to play their part with so much conviction only because they themselves had no chance of winning. Hinault noticed in the first stages that he was in far better form than he had expected, and because he had the egotism and ambition of a great champion, from that moment onwards he did everything he could to try to escape from his promise.

In the first Pyrenees stage he unleashed a furious attack that put him into the yellow jersey. LeMond, who was naive enough to think that Hinault would keep his word, kept watch over the peloton and thereby lost five-and-a-half minutes. That was a substantial gap, but Hinault knew how strong his team-mate was and felt far from secure. So, he launched a new attack the next day. He was no Jonathan Boyer and he knew LeMond could not afford to instigate a pursuit. This time, however, Hinault had overestimated his own strength; he suffered a major *défaillance* and lost almost five minutes to LeMond, who won the stage. Three stages later, though, Hinault went on the attack again.

LeMond had slowly begun to realise what his team-mate was up to and complained about this at length to the journalists. To do this was to break the peloton's oath of silence, and the majority of the La Vie Claire team turned against LeMond so sharply that he had to dine alone in his room that evening. A day later he captured the yellow jersey, but in the next stage he once again had to cope with an attack by Hinault. He was able to parry it, and at the base of the ascent to the stage finish at Alpe d'Huez, the two team-mates had a four-and-a-half minute lead on their pursuers. LeMond quite rightly did not trust Hinault even for a moment and wanted to drop him. Tapie personally nipped this in the bud. LeMond had done enough damage with his complaints to the media. To quash all rumours about divisions in the La Vie Claire team he instructed LeMond to stay with Hinault and go across the finish line with him hand in hand. LeMond obeyed and during the climb stayed at the wheel of Hinault, who determined the tempo.

At the top the two men did their best to turn the event into something inspirational. LeMond put his hand on Hinault's shoulder, although he would just as soon have had his guts for garters. Hinault, who had probably been silently praying that LeMond would puncture, just like Bartali in the Aosta stage of the 1949 Tour, raised his team-mate's arm high in triumph and released him just in time to cross the line in first place. Television images showed that at some point they even spoke to each other, something they hadn't done for days. In cycle racing little is needed to bring reporters into a state of delirium, and this bit of stage business by the two men was hailed as the most moving sports event of the year 1986. On Dutch television Mart Smeets burbled the following ecstatic words: 'What a gesture! *What* a gesture! Fantastic! This was fantastic! LeMond putting his arm on that shoulder! That smile! Oh, how beautiful this is! How beautiful sport can be! Oh! How splendid this is! It's fantastic to be seeing this! Oh! It's magnificent! It's fantastic!'

In spite of the brotherly love that apparently existed between the two riders, Hinault stated later that day that he would do everything he could to retake the yellow jersey from LeMond. Before the start of the decisive time trial he hissed at his team-mate: 'I'll get you yet!' In spite of these attempts at intimidation LeMond retained the yellow jersey into Paris. Even then Hinault did not accept defeat. He flatly claimed that without his promise to LeMond he could easily have won the Tour himself. He admitted that there had indeed been some misunderstanding about his way of riding, but that was only because not everyone had realised that he wanted to give his team-mate a much more valuable gift than a simple Tour victory. By his seeming resistance he wanted to impart 'character' to LeMond.

> Thanks to me Greg has become a very good rider. Later on he'll draw a lot of benefit from the psychological war I've waged against him. From now on he'll be capable of winning the toughest races. I've taught him a lot. In future he'll be able to defend himself on every terrain and that, too, he owes in part to me. I don't regret what I've done, because it was all for his own good.

In France, Hinault's fairy tales were regarded as gospel truth, and Jacques Goddet even wrote that two yellow jerseys should actually be awarded. In the United States people had eyes only for the victory by a compatriot. American TV networks battled for the right to televise the last stage, and afterwards LeMond was received at the White House by President Ronald Reagan.

LeMond was able to profit only partially from his triumph, because a terrible hunting accident in the spring of 1987 caused him to lose two seasons. His recovery proceeded so slowly that halfway through 1989 almost no one still believed he would make a comeback. Hinault could write cheekily in his memoirs that at some point LeMond would have to show what he could do *without* his help. What Hinault could not foresee was that his former team-mate would in that same season win the Tour as well as the world championship, something Hinault never managed to do.

The Big Money

When Joop Zoetemelk, riding in the Paris Six Days Race at the end of 1985, heard that he had won the prize for the most remarkable performance of the season and would therefore receive a cheque in the amount of 50,000 guilders (at that time about £11,000), he asked with an incredulous look on his face whether he had understood correctly: '*Fifty thousand guilders*?'

Such an amount would have been unimaginable just a short time earlier. For example, Sean Kelly got only £3,500 for winning the 1984 Super Prestige Pernod, a forerunner of the World Cup. His victory in the most important classic of the year, Paris–Roubaix, earned him no more than £1,200.

The size of the amount that Zoetemelk received for his performance in the world championship was a clear sign that the big-money era had finally dawned for bike racing. The salaries of the top racing cyclists in particular rose swiftly. In 1983, Renault paid Laurent Fignon only £20,000 after his Tour victory that year. Less than ten years later, Miguel Induráin earned more than £400,000, while Lance Armstrong's income from all sources after *his* first Tour victory was over $7 million, an amount that would be trebled within a few years.

For the riders the key aspect of this development was not only that they could earn more than before, but also that the major sources of their income had changed. These were no longer the appearance fees for criteriums and kermesses, but the salaries and bonuses they received from their employers.

It goes without saying, of course, that the steep rise in riders' salaries affected the relations between employers and employees. The sponsors paid a lot of money to have the riders wear their companies' jerseys, but this gave them the right to determine when, and where, the riders would compete. For the *domestiques* this meant that team discipline became noticeably stricter; for the top men it meant that they often had to complete a programme that taxed them much too heavily.

The most important reasons for *extra-sportif* sponsors to invest money in a cycling team are improving their image and increasing their brand recognition. The latter can be achieved fairly quickly. Before Tapie launched his cycling team, only 18 per cent of the French population had heard of La Vie Claire. Within eighteen months this had risen to 73 per cent. With this Tapie had reached his major goal; little scope existed for a further increase. He therefore disbanded his cycling team after three seasons and from then on concentrated on football. Only through his sports goods business, Look, which functioned as co-sponsor with Toshiba, did he remain involved in cycle racing. Most of Tapie's competitors withdrew rather less quickly, but as a rule their involvement did not last more than five or six years. Of the seventeen teams that had taken part in the 1985 Tour, no fewer than fifteen had disappeared from it by 1992. The bicycle manufacturers who acted as sponsors in the early days normally stayed in the sport for decades, and therefore were often prepared to invest in the future, for example by organising races for amateurs or training youths. A few *extra-sportif* companies followed their example, but most tried to get the quickest possible return on their investment. They could therefore rarely afford to build a team slowly, with the result that young riders were often overextended. Coppi, Bartali, Bobet, Anquetil, Merckx and Hinault dared only occasionally to participate in the Tour de France in the same season that they completed the Giro; and none of them was younger than 25 when he tried it for the first time. Because Renault was mounting a large-scale advertising campaign in Italy in 1984, yet did not want to neglect the French market, Laurent Fignon was forced to include both races in his schedule when he was still only 23. He completed both, but a few months later had to be operated on because of persistent tendinitis in his Achilles tendon. After this he never returned to his old level. By the time Erik Breukink was 25 he had already had to ride the Giro and the Tour in the same year on three occasions, which may have been one reason why he was never able to develop his enormous capabilities to the full.

x x x

By his willingness to give LeMond a $1 million three-year contract, Bernard Tapie became one of the great trailblazers for the coming of the big money, but he certainly did not cause it. He was not alone and not even the first in assessing the true value of the publicity opportunities offered by cycle racing in its new, globalised form. Francesco Moser's breaking of Merckx's world hour record in January 1984 provided a clear indication that sponsors were ready to invest much larger amounts than they had been earlier.

In 1983 Moser was 32 and seemed to have reached the end of his career. The mountains of the Giro had clearly been too tough for him that year, and he had failed to complete it. Moreover, because his last major victory dated back to 1980, the cycling press had already more or less written him off. Yet although he found climbing ever more difficult, on flat roads he was still very strong. Furthermore, he was just as ambitious as he had been at the start of his career. So, an international group consisting of the Italian pharmaceutical company Also-Enervit, the Belgian biscuit manufacturer LU, and the English snack-food producer Tuc, had enough confidence in him to put up a small fortune for the preparation of his attempt to break the world hour record.

In 1972 Eddy Merckx had prepared for his attempt at the record to the full extent his financial resources would allow. Yet in comparison with Moser his approach was extremely primitive. Moser subjected himself to a Spartan training regime supervised by a special team of experts who used the most modern methods and the most advanced equipment available. One of these experts was Professor Francesco Conconi, later notorious for doping, who had been experimenting with new performance-enhancing techniques for years, such as transfusions of one's own blood that had been quick-frozen several months before. Due partly to tricks of this kind – at the time they were not yet banned – Moser reached a condition that not only enabled him twice to improve the world hour record, but also brought him victories in Milan–San Remo and the Giro, races he had never won before. Merckx, too, had been accompanied by a team of physicians, but his preparation had lasted only a few weeks. Moreover, he had to interrupt it several times in order to fulfill race contracts.

The difference in approach is also evident from the equipment that the two used for their attempts to break the record. Ernesto Colnago, the designer of Merckx's bike, started from the self-evident notion that one rides faster when pushing less weight along.

Therefore he used super light-weight materials in which he had also drilled as many holes as possible.

Moser's bicycle builders did not have to depend on common sense. Instead they made use of a laboratory where they could carry out systematic scientific research. They found that stability and drag were much more important variables than weight. The final model (the tenth they built and tested) was four kilos heavier than Merckx's bike and had a completely different weight distribution. Moreover, it included several radical innovations, such as disc wheels of different sizes and a bullhorn bar.

Before 1984 sponsors did not make much effort to give their riders an advantage over their competitors by means of technical improvements. In 1979 Cyrille Guimard equipped his team with 'profile bicycles' that the Gitane factory had been able to develop thanks to the wind-tunnels and technical expertise provided by co-sponsor Renault, but the gain in time these bicycles made possible was minimal. Except during the period when the derailleur was introduced, it never made much difference to riders what bike they used. However, since the time the technical development of the bicycle could benefit from 'the big money', it has happened twice that a rider has won an important race partly through using superior equipment, namely the Giro of 1984 and the Tour of 1989. In both cases Laurent Fignon was the victim. It was ironic that his team director was the same Cyrille Guimard who had initiated the search for new technical possibilities.

x x x

The logical consequence of the rising salaries, and the obligation to provide riders with the most advanced equipment available, was that companies had to invest ever-increasing amounts in order to field a team that was likely to win. In 1970 the Mars-Flandria team, with Roger De Vlaeminck, Joop Zoetemelk, and world champion Jean-Pierre Monseré, cost only £60,000. Ten years later Renault had to pay close to eight times that amount for a team led by Bernard Hinault. Another ten years later the budget for teams like Panasonic and PDM was almost £3 million. Since that time these amounts have multiplied. This inflation means, of course, that only large firms can still afford to become the lead sponsors of teams capable of playing important roles in major races.

It goes without saying that businesses were willing to invest ever-larger amounts only because they assumed there would be an adequate pay-off. In this respect they put their faith especially in the effect of television images. Their impact developed relatively slowly in the 1960s and 1970s, but increased almost exponentially in the 1980s. This not only led to cycle racing becoming ever more attractive to advertisers, but meant above all that a fundamental change took place in the way cycling fans followed their favorite sport. Articles in newspapers and magazines, later combined with radio broadcasts, had long assumed a commanding position. Photos and films were, at most, illustrative. But once it became possible to televise an ever-larger part of the progress of the race, the visual image crowded out the written word so forcefully that a growing part of the public began to regard press accounts as superfluous. An important milestone in this development took place in 1985. In that year the French TV channel France 2 acquired the exclusive right to televise the stages of the Tour. The amount paid was greater than what *L'Equipe* and *Le Parisien Libéré* spent annually on organising the Tour. From the founding of the Tour de France, the management's key objective had always been to sell as many newspapers as possible, but now they gave their top priority to television. This change was made possible primarily by technological developments. Beginning in 1984 it became possible to use communications satellites. As a result, images of the Tour could suddenly be disseminated worldwide. In 1978, the year of Hinault's first victory, the arrival of the riders in Paris was watched by viewers in five countries. In 1986, the year *le blaireau*, the badger, took his leave, it had become 27. Fragments of Tour broadcasts were viewed even in nations with little or no tradition of cycle sport, such as Sri Lanka, Swaziland, Barbados, Botswana, Thailand, Puerto Rico, Nepal, Macao, China, Kenya, Saudi-Arabia, Taiwan, Pakistan, Hong Kong, and the Maldives. The total number of people who saw at least three minutes of the race was estimated at a billion. It hardly needs saying that this development suddenly made the Tour highly attractive to multinational sponsors. Thus Perrier and Vittel saw to their dismay that they were pushed aside by Coca-Cola, which in 1985 was willing, in exchange for a twelve-year contract, to pay sums that firms aiming almost exclusively at the French market could not possibly afford.

The chance of selling transmission rights throughout the entire world naturally served as a strong stimulus to the directors of France 2 to spare neither trouble nor expense in order to offer viewers the most attractive product possible. They were in fact forced to do so because state-owned broadcasters were facing ever greater competition from commercial channels that sometimes concentrated largely or wholly on sports. France 2 therefore took things in hand in the grand style. In the 1984 Tour, TV directors were embarrassed because the Belgian Fons de Wolf got so far ahead during a solo escape that it proved impossible to cover both the leader and the pursuing peloton with just one helicopter. From the next year on at least two or three helicopters were sent up to transmit images, so that in principle an awkward state of affairs like that could not happen again. Due to this large-scale commitment of material it also became possible during mountain stages, when the peloton broke wide open, not only to let the viewers see those at the front but also to show how much their less talented colleagues needed to exert themselves to get over the mountains. By placing ever more fixed cameras along the routes over the cols, other details that had been invisible up to that point could be brought into the picture. Aside from this huge expansion of technological resources, the length of the broadcasts increased markedly. In 1985 the number of hours the Tour was televised was approximately 55. Ten years later that number had doubled, and in 1998 a temporary peak of 130 hours was attained.

The advance of television naturally had far-reaching consequences for the print media. In the first half of the twentieth century bicycle road racing existed by the grace of the attention that newspapers were willing to give it. Riders needed journalists just as badly as the other way around. Usually they were very close to each other and shared each others' secrets. Beginning in the 1960s, the relationship became gradually more business-like. To the degree that a few words spoken before the TV camera were more important to sponsors than a long article in a sports journal, this tendency continued. Bernard Tapie was a pioneer in this respect, too, instructing his top riders in principle to give interviews only to television and glossy magazines such as *Paris-Match*. Naturally other cyclists also adopted this attitude as soon as they achieved star status. Thus the Dane, Bjarne Riis, who had always been very approachable for journalists as long as he was just a 'minor rider', never had time any more once he had won the Tour. It became all but impossible to elicit serious comments from him.

The sportswriters at *L'Equipe* who, like their predecessors at *L'Auto*, had always enjoyed a privileged position, were confronted with the new power relationship in a very painful fashion when they discovered during the 1985 Tour that they could no longer get rooms in the same hotel as Goddet and Lévitan. Their place was taken by reporters, technicians, and other employees of France 2. Seven years later they lost further ground: the organisational work performed by *L'Equipe* and *Le Parisien Libéré* was taken over by the *Société du Tour de France*, which in turn was part of the Amaury Sports Organisation. These developments did not, of course, mean that the role of sportswriters was completely played out after 1992. Although they see the same images as the viewing public, their expertise and the contacts they have still enable them to tell a story about the race that does not appear on the TV screen. But that does not change the fact that the press now takes a back seat.

Two cyclists best symbolised the arrival of an age in which the image had replaced the spoken and written word. The first was Mario Cipollini, the perfect showman, whose talents would have been largely wasted in the pre-television era. Like no other rider he knew how to exploit the possibilities of the new medium, not only by his spectacular sprints, during which he usually glanced briefly over his shoulder at his defeated rivals, but also because he came up with some new gimmick in just about every race. These were rarely if ever striking comments; instead they were new touches to his appearance or clothing that were sometimes extraordinarily creative. None of the world champions who preceded him had ever hit on the idea of applying the rainbow colours – emblematic of the world championship – to his shorts or shoes. Cipollini's innovations were usually in complete conflict with the regulations, but knowing that he had once again gained valuable publicity he happily paid the fines.

Whereas Cipollini symbolised the dominant position that the image had secured, the forced retreat of the word was personified by the rider who dominated the Tour during the first half of the 1990s, the Spaniard Miguel Induráin. Time and again he drove reporters and sportswriters to despair as they tried to pry a newsworthy remark from his mouth. He made no secret of his extreme dislike of interviews. Once he even let slip that he did not want to learn French because then he would have to cope with even more questions. Of course Induráin's attitude owed much to his very special personality. But people are generally able to adapt if it is genuinely necessary. Joop Zoetemelk, for example, at first faced the microphone every bit as uncomfortably and cluelessly as the Spaniard, but felt compelled to improve his performance. At the end of his career he was fully capable of giving a decent interview in French or Dutch, even if his unmistakable progress was insufficient to bring him the position in radio or TV that he once said was his ambition. Induráin made absolutely no effort to follow in Zoetemelk's footsteps and was not pushed to do so by his sponsor. The latter was fully satisfied with the constant attention the cameramen paid to Induráin and the thousands of times the company's name appeared on the screen.

It was not only because of his lack of talkativeness that Induráin fits his period so superbly. He may well have been the first star who did not need to make any concessions for the sake of his image in the press, as a result of which he could subordinate everything to his ultimate goal: a victory in the Tour. In contrast to what is often assumed, he was by no means a late bloomer. He was Spanish junior champion, and at the age of nineteen the youngest rider in history to wear the leader's jersey in the Tour of Spain. Two years later, in 1986, he duelled with Erik Breukink, the other great hope of his generation, in the Tour de l'Avenir and beat him in the time trial and the final classification. After that, little was heard of him for several years aside from a handful of wins in minor Spanish tours. While Breukink used up his physical capital as a racing cyclist, Induráin hid himself in the peloton and used only the interest on his athletic endowment. Initially he appeared as Pedro Delgado's chief *domestique*, and only when his capacities were fully developed did he set his sights on a Tour victory. He took it for the first time in 1991. That same year Breukink clearly began to decline.

Once Induráin had reached the top he continued to show the same discipline with which he had built his career. The organisers of the Vuelta a España tried very hard to tempt the best Spanish rider of all time to enter their tour, but in vain. Induráin had figured out for himself that participation in the Giro d'Italia served as a better preparation for the Tour de France than did the Vuelta, where after 1991 he was seen no more. Nor did he try to make himself conspicuous in the major classics. His most important sponsors, the management of Banesto, made no attempt to change his mind. Market research had shown that three-quarters of the attention of the Spanish public was focused on the Tour, the remaining quarter on the Vuelta, and that other races mattered very little.

In the Tour, too, Induráin was seldom if ever prepared to make accommodating gestures. Sportswriters had to be satisfied with his willingness to cut a cake on his birthday, which always took place during the Tour, but were never able to get him to eat even so much as a crumb. After all, it didn't fit into the carefully balanced diet he observed. For the same reason he merely moistened his lips with the champagne offered to him, wiping them immediately afterwards with a handkerchief. The same principle distinguished his way of riding. Even the infrequent attacks he launched seemed invariably to have been subjected to a careful cost-benefit analysis. This tactic unquestionably best suited his mental attitude, but he had other reasons for it as well. First of all, while it is true that he possessed enormous physical resources, he also had a handicap. He weighed 79-80 kilos, and therefore had to wage a battle with gravity on every col, and yet, he hardly needed to defer to the best climbers of his era. Eddy Merckx, who at the end of his career had ever more trouble hauling his 73 kilos over the mountains, was not entirely wrong in saying that Induráin was a wonder of nature. The only problem for 'Big Mig' was that he used much more energy during the climbs than his more slenderly built colleagues. As it was, he did have lots of energy, and if the ascents were not too steep, or if he got sufficient opportunity to recuperate between mountain stages, he could easily compensate for this vulnerability. But in races like the 1994 Tour, with its five successive Alpine stages, he always ran the risk that his strength would fail him a day earlier than his rivals' did. Economy was therefore the rule. He did not care one whit, of course, that for this reason he was more than once accused of a lack of *panache*.

Induráin's calculating method of riding was often criticised, but he was by no means the only champion guilty of it. Most especially in Italy this tactic was widely used, and Gianni Bugno's victory in the 1990 Giro showed great similarity to Induráin's victories in the Tour. This was no coincidence. Both riders, after all, had to meet different demands than those that faced the champions of the past. Riders such as Coppi and Bartali received a relatively low salary from the companies for which they raced, and drew their income mostly from appearance fees whose size was determined not only by their performances but also by the way they were depicted. For example, they had to be able to inspire journalists to lyrical heights by undertaking solo rides and spectacular attacks. Moreover, they paid their *domestiques* partly from their own pockets, either directly, or indirectly by taking them along to criteriums. For this reason, too, they could, by and large, decide for themselves which races they would take part in and how to ride their races.

From the moment the big money made its entry into cycle sport, the position of the stars shifted significantly. In exchange for the millions they received in salary, they were forced to surrender much of their independence. They fulfilled a clearly specified function in a team which had a strict division of labour, accompanied by team directors, mechanics, masseurs, physicians, public relations officials, even psychologists. On the one hand this made their task easier, but on the other it significantly increased their responsibility. If a top rider failed, it was much more than a personal defeat. It also meant that the financiers' investments and the exertions of his entire team had largely been for nothing. Specialists in one-day races could still afford to take more risks. After a defeat, they generally had an early opportunity to try again. Even if they fell short in the spring, they could often make up for it in the Tour, where a resounding stage win has at least as much publicity value as a triumph in a classic. But riders who were signed up to excel in a major tour did not have this kind of escape available to them. If, like LeMond, Induráin, or Lance Armstrong, they staked their whole season on the Tour or the Giro and did not meet expectations, the entire team's cycling year could be written off as a failure.

It is no wonder, therefore, that the favourites in the Tour or Giro have generally proceeded ever more carefully. This sometimes leads to race tactics that closely resemble the notorious *catenaccio* system of football, pioneered in Italy, which featured a stifling defence (*catenaccio* is a bolt on a door). The hope for a victory is often completely overshadowed by the fear of a loss. All risks are to be avoided. Every unnecessary exertion is forbidden, especially because the differences in strength are so small. This type of riding flourished first in Italy, which with respect to high salaries was way ahead. Already in the 1980s it led former world champion Moreno Argentin to say: 'We don't ride to win but to let our opponents lose.'

Fortunately for cycle sport, the *catenaccio* system has never been all-inclusive, and there are always riders who don't want to keep to the unwritten rules. This can be very risky, but at the same time they force their opponents to react to unforeseen situations. Thus Induráin's most dangerous rivals were not men like Gianni Bugno or Toni Rominger, who tried to beat the Spanish champion with his own weapons, nor even the gifted climber Marco Pantani, whose predictable attacks in the mountains could not possibly compensate for his losses in the time trials. A much greater problem for Induráin was the physically less well-endowed Claudio Chiappucci because he was quite irrational. In the flat stages he sprinted away on every slope that yielded points for the mountain prize, a superfluous exertion that no *catenaccio*-adherent would ever risk undertaking. Moreover, he launched escapes during flat stages, thereby risking a senseless waste of strength because of the overwhelmingly likelihood of the peloton reeling him in. Still wilder was his attack in 1992 during the Alpine stage from Saint Gervais to Sestriere in Italy, when he took off 180 kilometres from the finish without having team-mates along who could give him support. Not only did Chiappucci secure victory in the stage but he also succeeded in leading Induráin astray, something that rarely happened. When the Spaniard tried to bring back the Italian during the last ascent, he had clearly overestimated his resources and even suffered something of a *défaillance*. This moment of weakness did not have any consequences, though, because none of Induráin's other rivals was able or willing to follow Chiappucci's example.

With his long solo ride Chiappucci not only won the stage but he scored another victory as well. There was not a shadow of a doubt that, outside Spain, he ranked much higher in the public's favour than Induráin. His popularity grew even more when journalists discovered that Chiappucci's mother had gone to Lourdes during the Tour to pray for her son. This gave the Italian cyclist precisely that human-interest element for which press and television looked to Induráin in vain. It was therefore no surprise that the presence of Chiappucci and his mother – who often fired the starting pistol – was more important to the organisers of criteriums than the participation of the Tour victor. In the golden age of criterium races, Chiappucci would unquestionably have earned more money than Induráin. But in the early 1990s he was almost an anachronism.

In the eyes of most viewers, Chiappucci's sudden attacks were the few exciting elements in what had become very monotonous Tours. Time after time, Induráin defeated his rivals so resoundingly during the first time trial that the further progress of the Tour held scarcely any surprises. Yet his victories were significantly less straightforward than appeared at first sight. Unfortunately for the organisers, the most interesting aspects of his triumphs were not captured on the screen and could only be enlarged upon in the print media. On the one hand, it was clear to every viewer that Induráin succeeded time and again in keeping all possible uncertainties to a minimum. On the other hand, the tactical masterpieces that were necessary to accomplish this stayed out of the picture. The biggest problem confronting Induráin was that his team was relatively weak and not able fully to control the way the race unfolded. No matter how strong he was, he would not have been able to hold his own against a tightly-knit coalition. He could only prevent close cooperation among his competitors by playing them off against each other and by giving each a share of the spoils. Induráin was better at this than anybody else. He had none of Merckx's cannibalistic tendencies. The only thing that really interested him was winning the Tour. He was therefore fully ready to focus on the general classification and to distribute stage wins and mountain prizes to other riders with a generous hand. This was one of the aspects in which he differed from Anquetil, who was often regarded as his model. Like Induráin, Anquetil had the reputation of being a master calculator, but to ensure his market value in criteriums from time to time he felt obliged to win mountain stages or undertake insane ventures, such as the Dauphiné Libéré and Bordeaux–Paris 'double'. For Induráin this was not necessary. The only thing he had to do was win the Tour, and that was a task he carried out to perfection.

However many subtle refinements Induráin's victories may have embodied, the Tour's organisers probably breathed a sigh of relief when the 1996 Tour, in which his dominance finally came to an end, demonstrated clearly recognizable patterns: major collapses, spectacular attacks, and an unforeseen course of events. Jan Ullrich's victory in 1997 also encompassed more dramatic moments than Induráin's last triumphs.

The Tour in which Induráin was finally beaten was noteworthy in another way: Bjarne Riis was the first Dane to wear the yellow jersey into Paris, just as the following year Ullrich was the first

German. These successes not only inspired great public enthusiasm in both these countries but also attracted new sponsors. The dream of Lévitan and Goddet to popularise the Tour beyond the classic cycling countries, seemed to be coming ever closer to realisation. International political and economic events also contributed to this development. The collapse of the Communist bloc had the result that riders from countries like the former GDR, Russia, Latvia, Lithuania, Poland, Ukraine, Uzbekistan and Kazakhstan had opportunities to match themselves against Western European professionals. At the same time the field of participants in the Tour expanded in other directions as well. A solid contingent of American, British, Australian, New Zealand and Colombian riders came into being; and some from Brazil, Venezuela and Mexico turned up from time to time. It is obvious that the arrival of riders from all points of the compass was matched by greater interest among the public in their countries of origin.

x x x

At the conclusion of the 1997 season, Tour director Jean-Marie Leblanc had every reason to be most pleased. His Tour, which from an economic point of view had been at the edge of the abyss time and again until the 1980s, had become a profitable enterprise on a global scale. It now earned so much money that teams did not need to pay entry fees any more and riders were housed much more commodiously than had ever been the case before. The only dark side for cycle sport was that the Tour de France was so successful that almost all the other races were in danger of being pushed aside. Even the Giro was clearly a second-tier race. For years Italian teams had scarcely gone beyond their own borders, but they could no longer afford to stay at home and contended just as vigorously for permission to enter the French Tour as did teams from other countries. As the costs of organising races kept going up – if only to pay the policemen who kept the roads clear – it became ever harder to find enough sponsors to balance the budget. Some races with an illustrious past, such as Paris–Nice, were in a precarious state. Yet nobody worried much about that. Thanks to the Tour's enormous attraction to sponsors, it was strong enough to carry the whole of cycle sport by itself. Less than a year would pass before it became apparent that the position of the Tour de France was much more vulnerable than at first glance it seemed to be.

Fuelled by Dynamite

On 14 July 1998, as the Tour reached French soil three days after its start in Ireland, the mood was exceptionally festive. Not only was it the national holiday, but less than 48 hours earlier France had become world champion in football for the first time in history. After the final whistle, hundreds of thousands of people had streamed into the streets, and a euphoria that awoke memories of the Liberation held sway. Moreover, this success fed a feeling of invincibility that was expressed on many banners. There seemed to be a new élan that would, for the first time in thirteen years, inevitably bring a Frenchman to Paris wearing the yellow jersey. Which cyclist that had to be was clear to all. It was Richard Virenque, who had already won the mountain prize three times and, in the previous year, had finished second behind Jan Ullrich. With his abilities as a time trialist, the German was still the top favourite, but thanks to a well-coordinated offensive Virenque's strong Festina team had seriously threatened Ullrich in the Alps in 1997. Because this time Virenque was surrounded by an even stronger team as a result of the engagement of Alex Zülle, twice winner of the Tour of Spain, and because there were also serious doubts about the effectiveness of Ullrich's preparation, a French victory seemed imminent.

The prologue, a short time trial, gave every reason for optimism. Three members of the Festina team finished among the top ten, and Virenque lost only five seconds to Ullrich. All the same, the team's accomplishments were threatened by a dark shadow. Near Lille a team attendant, Willy Voet, had been arrested with large quantities of EPO (erythropoietin), growth hormones, testosterone, and corticoids in his car. Initially the team's director, Bruno Roussel, tried to persuade journalists that this must be the result of a misunderstanding because all the team's support staff were in Dublin. He knew this was untrue, of course, but he still remained quite convinced the whole affair would be hushed up. The same was true of his riders, who were mainly worried that they would

137

not get their essential drugs on time. Nor did Willy Voet imagine, at first, that the issue was going to assume major proportions. During his interrogation he dropped the names of Virenque and of Bernadette Chirac, wife of the President, who had received the Festina team three weeks earlier. The year before, this tactic would unquestionably have worked, but this time it made no impression at all. The Tour has a special status in France and has long been pretty much above the law. As the French journal *Libération* later revealed, during the 1990s more than one doping affair had been swept under the carpet on orders from on high. But this time things were different. One reason why Henri Desgrange and Jacques Goddet had always been able to count on the government's benevolence was that they maintained strict political neutrality. The new owner of the Tour, Philippe Amaury, was less circumspect. In 1995 he actively supported the presidential campaign of Jacques Chirac, who was indeed elected but then lost the parliamentary elections of May 1997. The new Minister of Youth and Sport, the Communist Marie-George Buffet, announced immediately after her entry into office that she wanted to deal with doping in a thoroughgoing way. Although there is absolutely no reason to doubt her sincerity and to dismiss the intervention of the authorities in the Festina affair as merely an act of political revenge, it is clear that at a critical moment the Tour could no longer count on government protection.

It took a while before people in the cycling world began to realise that the Tour de France was no longer unassailable. Jean-Marie Leblanc sought to turn the tide by expelling the Festina team from the Tour, but that gave little relief. Nobody responded to his plea to let the Tour management and the cycling federation deal with the rest of the affair. Nor was Leblanc able to prevent the arrest, first of Roussel and then of the entire Festina team. Except for Virenque and Pascal Hervé, all the riders at once confessed, and admitted having used stimulants. Their confessions were front-page news and pushed all other accounts of the race to the inside pages. An appeal to the media by Patrick Lefevere, the Mapei team director, asking them to give the doping affair a rest for the time being and to return to the sporting aspects, was quite pointless. In the days when cyclists and journalists were still in a kind of symbiotic relationship, Lefevere's words would probably have found an audience. But since then the situation had changed radically. The various TV channels competed to portray the intervention by the police and the judicial system as sensationally as possible. France 2 actually went so far as to send reporters to the hotels where the teams were staying, in order to examine the contents of garbage bags for evidence of doping. The riders' outrage over this lack of loyalty by the broadcaster, which by virtue of its monopoly of the transmissions surely had an interest in a smooth progression of the race, led to a two-hour strike the next day.

Some hope dawned for the Tour management when yellow-jersey wearer Jan Ullrich, who seemed to be heading for an uncontested second straight victory, was deposed by the Italian climber Marco Pantani during a cold, rainy Alpine stage in a manner reminiscent of a similar coup by Charly Gaul 30 years before. For a moment, stories about doping scandals seemed to have been pushed aside. But the management's cautious optimism melted away very quickly. A few days earlier judicial authorities had announced that more than a hundred vials of EPO had been found in a car belonging to the TVM team in the spring. Twenty-four hours after Pantani's solo ride, the police raided the team's Albertville hotel and detained the six surviving members of the team until the small hours. The next day the 1998 Tour almost came to an end. After 30 kilometres the peloton came to a halt and the riders took off their numbers. Three teams left for home, while the rest of the peloton arrived in Aix-les-Bains several hours behind schedule. The TVM team was allowed to cross the finish line in first place, but the day's results were cancelled.

The riders were not the only ones to be outraged. Members of the National Assembly asked questions. The Dutch and Belgian cycling federations made a joint protest to the French Ministry of Justice. The former Olympic skiing champion, Jean-Claude Killy, president of the *Société du Tour de France*, who was staying in the same time hotel as TVM, stated that the police had treated the riders as if they were criminals. The French magistrates' union countered this by pointing out that police behaviour had been correct and that the cyclists had received exactly the same treatment as other detainees. They were right, but for many *that* was the biggest shock, namely that Tour de France riders, who had once all been gods, could no longer expect special treatment. Even the unspoken threat that this might bring the Tour de France to an untimely end seemed to have no effect. Marie-George Buffet stated that if a Tour without doping were impossible, then the Tour would just have to disappear. Law officers showed themselves to be equally unimpressed and authŏrised a further raid the day after the peloton's protest action. The result was that three more teams quit the race. The peloton that finally reached Paris comprised only 96 of the 189 who had started in Dublin. Furthermore, the peloton's arrival on the Champs Elysées did not mean that the affair was over and done with. In September *France Soir* published a detailed account of the confessions that members of the Festina team had made. A good half year later, Willy Voet published a book that revealed the doping practices of the peloton in great detail. As well as that, leading actors in the drama, like Virenque and Festina team director Bruno Roussel, published accounts of *their* views concerning the affair.

Police and officers of the court had met no resistance to speak of when they invaded the world of the Tour. Yet the judicial authorities had certainly not gained a complete victory. The judicial campaign was not only about a precise observance of the law: a political struggle was also taking place, with the public's favour as the key stake at issue. That cyclists, team directors, and organisers would make an appeal to the sentiments of the millions who followed the Tour on television or in the newspapers was predictable: it was the only way in which they could defend themselves. But the police and the courts did not adopt a different approach. Television channels received one tip after another so that a raid might appear on the screen, magistrates gave press conferences and submitted to lengthy media interviews, convinced that they were right. In spite of this they enjoyed little success. They could not complain about lack of publicity, and the many letters to the editor in which correspondents expressed their abhorrence of doping indicates that the judicial authorities had many people on their side. Yet it was simply not the case that the public turned massively against the Tour. Viewer numbers did not drop, and this time, too, millions of people came from far and wide to cheer on the passing caravan. On the Champs Elysées people paid homage to Marco Pantani as though nothing had happened during the preceding weeks. Even during the protest action between Albertville and Aix-les-Bains, the thousands of spectators who had turned up for nothing did not take out their anger on the riders. On the contrary, the caravan was greeted with loud applause. Instead everything that smacked of officialdom was showered with abuse. Even the completely guiltless organisers, who would have been more than happy to have swept the matter under the carpet, were jeered and spat upon. Jean-Marie Leblanc called it the worst day of his life as Tour director. And yet, he had every reason to be pleased. The Tour could easily survive having a few teams leave for home, but it would have been finished had the sponsors departed as well. That would have been far from impossible *if* the overwhelming majority of the public had not supported the riders so emphatically.

x x x

The hostile attitude that the great majority of the public showed towards the police action unquestionably disappointed the politicians who were involved. Yet they ought to have known better. Doping is as old as sport itself, and cycling fans never got very excited about it. Racing cyclists had initially not even found it necessary to keep it a secret. Soon after Paris–Rouen in 1869, there was an open discussion in the press as to which substances were most effective in enhancing performance. In the period when long-distance races such as Paris–Brest–Paris were first organised, there were companies that advertised products like *l'Elixir de vitesse* or *Vélo Guignolet*, which probably consisted largely of caffeine, cocaine or morphine. Around the turn of the century, European riders who participated in six-day races in the United States returned with American Coffee, a concoction that aside from large quantities of caffeine also contained ether, strychnine, cocaine and even nitroglycerine. Indeed, as people said at the time, riders were almost literally fuelled by dynamite.

The use of these substances occurred in complete openness. At the end of the nineteenth century the English manager 'Choppy' Warburton even made it a custom during track races to prepare his 'magical potions' with an excess of mysterious gestures in order to hand them to his riders while running at full speed, with the crowd cheering him on.

Doping moved into the realm of the semi-clandestine only when the popularity of cycle racing came to be increasingly based on the heroic representations given to it. The giants of the road were deemed to owe their feats exclusively to perseverance and muscular strength; and that they might at times resort to chemical means was a subject not to be spoken about too openly. Yet it was hardly a secret. When Henri Desgrange drafted new contracts with the participants in the Tour in 1930, he actually found it necessary to put into writing that the organisation would provide for normal medical care, but that the cost of 'stimulants, tonics, and doping' had to be paid by the riders themselves. Now and then articles also appeared in the press with so many details about the way in which riders 'looked after' themselves that no one needed to be under any illusions. In the 1920s, during that famous interview with Albert Londres, the Pélissier brothers showed him a large supply of pills and cocaine. After the war there were a good many more such 'confessions'. From time to time, even major champions were extraordinarily expansive. Thus Coppi admitted in an interview that he used *la bomba* – amphetamine – only when necessary, but that it was almost always necessary. A few years later Anquetil was even less reticent. In a series of question-and-answer sessions with *France Dimanche* he stated not only that he himself had regularly used illicit drugs but also that riders who claimed not to be doing so were either imbeciles or hypocrites.

Although there was sufficient information available to provide a reasonably reliable insight into drug use in the peloton, this scarcely affected the image of the sport. The 'revelations' by the Pélissiers did absolutely nothing to harm the picture of incredibly courageous riders who had to meet almost superhuman demands under the most dire conditions. On the contrary, it was precisely due to the interview with the Pélissiers that the myth of 'forced labourers of the road' found general acceptance. Nor was Coppi's reputation harmed by his frankness. Although his comments were confirmed by several riders and it is even known exactly how many pills he had taken when he lowered the world hour record in 1942, most articles and books about Coppi are silent about his doping, deny it, or represent it as an act of desperation he resorted to during the last years of his career, when his strength increasingly deserted him. Sportswriters, in fact, rarely felt any desire to put the issue of doping front and centre. Of course, on the whole they knew very well that the image they presented to the outside world distorted the way things were, but they simply had no interest in describing it more realistically. After all, they also profited from the mythological depiction of cycle racing. Besides, in the period before 'the big money' entered the scene, they were so close to the riders that they normally felt a strong solidarity with them. If a cyclist became a bit too loose-tongued they usually, almost automatically, protected him from himself, however much news value his remarks might have been worth. Thus Pierre Chany, cycling editor for *L'Equipe*, expressed dismay when he read the question-and-answer sessions with Anquetil in *France Dimanche* and stated at once that he had 'urged Jacques so strongly to exercise caution, since his interviewer did not belong to the milieu'.

Although the negative aspects of cycle racing were papered over pretty effectively, this was not the main reason for the compliant position generally taken on doping. The chief reason was the attitude of the public. It was always the myths and legends that lent bicycle road racing such an enormous appeal. Most cycling fans were interested only in information that confirmed these mythological images or embellished them even more. If journalists had tried to disturb this dream, the public would undoubtedly have treated them with the same hostility they directed towards the authorities during the Festina affair. Of course information emerged from time to time that did not square with the idea of 'the giants of the road', but there has never been a lack of defence mechanisms to neutralise it. Even when it was no longer possible to deny that doping took place, or to ignore it, it could always still be rationalised. The riders themselves contributed enough data to make this possible. The Pélissiers justified the use of drugs by pointing to the hardships to which they were exposed. Anquetil later embroidered the same theme, and in his interview with *France Dimanche* he claimed that even the most talented rider could not possibly compete in races like the Tour, the Dauphiné Libéré, or Bordeaux–Paris aided by mineral water alone. Arguments like these are evidently sufficiently persuasive for it often to be claimed nowadays, in all seriousness, that shorter stages and more rest days in the Tour will prove effective in preventing doping. None other than Marie-George Buffet showed herself to believe this piece of received wisdom, and during the Festina affair she urged Jean-Marie Leblanc to make the route of future Tours less onerous. Leblanc agreed, though against his better judgment, because as an ex-rider he knew all too well that measures of this kind fail utterly to get to the core of the problem. To be able to complete a long, demanding tour without extreme weight loss or damage to one's health, a sound preparation and nutrition are essential, but not amphetamines, anabolic steroids, growth hormones or EPO. Such products are taken only to win or, at the very least, to be able to compete at a high level. As Goddet said, drugs are taken to ride 3,500 kilometres in twenty days for the same reason that they are taken to run the 100-metre sprint in less than ten seconds.

x x x

If the cycling world had succeeded in keeping its ranks more or less closed, the phenomenon of doping would never have been more than an insignificant footnote. Riders didn't want to talk about it, journalists didn't want to write about it, and the public didn't want to hear about it. In fact, all parties were in agreement that the use of stimulants was perhaps regrettable, but that up to a certain point it was tolerable. Hardly anybody spoke of combating it. In the 1950s the situation gradually changed. This did not originate from within the cycling milieu itself; the opposite was the case. More and more outside pressure was applied to deal effectively with doping practices. According to the sociologist Rudolf Stokvis there were two main reasons for this. In the first place there was the mistrust with which the western authorities regarded the achievements of athletes from countries in the East bloc, which after the 1952 Olympic Games in Helsinki increasingly used sporting success as an item of prestige. Next were the activities of sports physicians who wanted to protect their monopoly over the practice of medicine against the non-medically schooled trainers who had moved into their territory.

It is surely no coincidence that the man who gained the nickname *Monsieur anti-doping* in cycle racing was a medical man, Pierre Dumas. In 1955, his first year as a Tour physician, he was at once confronted with several clear cases of doping during the Marseille-Avignon stage, when the riders went over Mont Ventoux. The Frenchman Jean Malléjac was barely saved from death. Dumas who, aside from his part-time appointment as a Tour physician, had no ties to cycling, had no earthly reason to keep the affair under wraps. He held a press conference in which he stated that he was prepared to recommend a charge of attempted murder.

In the years that followed, cycle racing was plagued on a number of occasions by incidents that could not possibly be kept hidden. Thus the Danish cyclist, Knud Enemark Jensen, fell off his bike and died during the road race in the 1960 Olympics. His death was widely attributed to an overdose of drugs, but since there was no autopsy there were no grounds for more than very strong suspicion. Five years later there was another scandal, as millions of TV viewers could see how the French favourites, Charly Grosskost and André Bayssière, climbing the Tourmalet during the Tour de l'Avenir, veered from side to side, smiling seraphically, and had to drop out shortly afterwards. Dr Dumas found a large supply of amphetamine and other stimulants in their luggage, and this time, too, he was unwilling to keep his mouth shut.

In various western European countries, scandals of this kind constituted the chief reason to move swiftly to adopt anti-doping legislation. The proposed statute that was introduced in the Belgian Senate in 1965 began with the statement that it was 'prohibited for participants in bicycle races or other sports competitions to avail themselves of stimulating agents'. It is completely understandable that cyclists protested vigorously against the implication that they were the chief sinners. That suggestion was, in fact, removed from the final draft, but this did not alter the fact that all over Western Europe bicycle racing was the chief target of the anti-doping campaign. The officials of the UCI and other federations had remarkably few illusions about the use of stimulants in the peloton, and in order to forestall the inevitable negative publicity, they tried to resist the law and its implementation as much as possible. They had scant success, since they were poorly organised and had few connections in political circles. The highest authority in the cycling world did not rest with the federations but with the organisers of the most important races. Thus it never cost Goddet and Lévitan much effort to get the UCI to toe the line. But now that the sport needed a strong central body to protect itself against outside intervention, as football, tennis, and athletics had succeeded in doing, it was almost powerless. The efforts of the Belgian cycling federation to stave off the inevitable as long as possible were easily crushed by the authorities by means of a large-scale raid at the start of Ghent-Wevelgem in March 1965. Nor did the resistance against the new regulations have much effect in France. The first inspection took place on 28 June 1966, at the end of the Tour stage from Royan to Bordeaux, less than four weeks after the new anti-doping statute had come into effect. Accompanied by the police, two physicians visited the hotels where the teams were staying and examined six riders. The two medical men evidently felt somewhat embarrassed and therefore not only collected urine samples but also conducted hasty medical examinations. In spite of this not notably credible attempt to persuade the riders that this was mainly about their health, there was a good deal of commotion in the peloton. The next day the race was stopped after five kilometres, on Anquetil's instigation, and everyone dismounted. The looming strike was broken by the reigning world champion, Tommy Simpson, who after several minutes seized his bicycle and rode off. Simpson involuntarily rendered the drug hunters a much greater service a year later, when he collapsed during the ascent of Mont Ventoux, due in part to overuse of stimulants and, in spite of Dumas's intervention, died moments later. From that point onwards open resistance was pointless.

The stimulant most used in the 1960s was amphetamine. Because this is easy to trace, the first doping tests were pretty accurate, and the number of cyclists who were caught was fairly high. According to Jean-Marie Leblanc, the 1968 Tour, in which he himself participated, was the only one in history to be really 'clean'. Whether that was actually the case is very much open to doubt. Dr Dumas said the Italian riders had discovered by this time that combining a diuretic pill with the injection of water into the bladder was a perfect way of eliminating traces of banned substances. But even if Leblanc was right, the effectiveness of the controls was in any case of very short duration. It did not prove difficult to stay ahead of the drug hunters, and riders soon found products that were easily masked or whose use could not be verified. For example, not until 1999 were laboratories able to trace corticoids, which became every bit as popular in the 1970s as amphetamine had been in the 1960s, and then only if they had been administered in synthetic form. EPO was introduced into the world of sports in 1987 and was widespread by 1993, but its use could not be traced until 2000. Growth hormones have been used for more than twenty years without fear of detection.

x x x

It is self-evident that reports about the inadequacy of inspections seriously challenged confidence in the anti-doping regime. Its credibility was undermined in other ways as well. The leadership of the national and international federations was in a difficult position. Their most important task was to do all they could to look after the interests of riders, sponsors, and all those directly involved in cycle sport. They realised only too well that an uncompromising hunt for stimulants hardly coincided with that task, and so they tried to control the hunt as much as possible. On the other hand, they could not openly sabotage the international policy on doping. The only way of resolving these conflicting demands was to find a precarious balance between forceful language and a highly flexible attitude. The first to profit from this was Eddy Merckx. When he tested positive during the 1969 Giro the regulations called for a month's suspension. This would have meant that he could not make his long-awaited debut in the Tour, which would have been a minor disaster from a commercial point of view. In the Belgian's honour the organisers had actually routed a stage through the small town where his parents had a business! Fortunately, the UCI saw a way out. Merckx had sworn that he had not used banned substances, and just this once the authorities decided to give him the benefit of the doubt. This greatly angered cyclists who had denied their offence just as forcefully but were penalised all the same, such as former Tour winners Jan Janssen and Roger Pingeon. The latter, especially, had every right to be bitter because he finished the Tour in second place behind Merckx.

The way in which the UCI resolved the Merckx-affair made it clear that the cycling authorities were far from insensitive to 'political' arguments. No wonder, then, that many people were easily persuaded that 1977 Tour winner Bernard Thévénet had been caught using stimulants, but that the doctors had swept the business under the rug. The fact, too, that seven-times world cyclo-cross champion, Eric De Vlaeminck, had to undergo detoxification in order to kick his amphetamine habit when he retired, although he had never tested positive, strengthened the public in the opinion that the examiners were far from honest. No wonder, then, that a rider who *was* found guilty was often regarded as a victim, or an unlucky devil, more than as a cheater. This was all too clear in the case of Michel Pollentier in 1978. He was caught red-handed at the conclusion of the Tour stage up to Alpe d'Huez, when he tried to bamboozle the examining doctor by filling a lab bottle with urine he had smuggled into the medical station in a condom (usually described euphemistically as a 'pear-shaped rubber bulb'). Although no one could doubt his guilt he was showered with expressions of sympathy, and on the occasions during his suspension when he was allowed to fire the starting pistol at criteriums, he was generally cheered more loudly than those who were racing.

The attitude adopted by the great majority of the European cycling public towards doping was so firmly rooted in tradition that even the Festina affair was scarcely able to change it. During the first few weeks afterwards it did happen that riders were jeered and sworn at when they were out training, but they had little or nothing to fear from those cycling fans who came to watch the races. When the Festina riders took their bow at the start of the Tour of Spain in September 1998, they got even more applause than the teams from the home country. New scandals such as raids in Belgium and Italy hardly affected this attitude, as became apparent from market research done by Nestlé in 2001. The Swiss firm was launching Aquarel, a new brand of mineral water, and was considering a contract with the Tour organisation. To learn the extent to which the many stories about the use of stimulants had damaged the image of cycle sport, the company sponsored surveys in several different countries. From these it emerged that the effect of all the recent revelations was virtually zero, so that the company's directors could confidently pay two million euros for their contract.

Thanks to the public's reaction, the damage done by the Festina affair remained limited for the time being. The problem was that this tolerant attitude could be found only in the classic cycling countries. That did not matter to Nestlé, because initially it planned to market Aquarel only in France, Belgium, Luxembourg, Spain, Portugal, and Germany. But images of the Tour are scattered all over the globe, and the great majority of the one to two billion viewers often have a different perception of cycling than prevails in Western Europe. For example, during the stage from Le Bourg d'Oisans to Courchevel in the 1997 Tour, Richard Virenque received Jan Ullrich's permission to win the stage in exchange for a certain sum of money. That the two had reached an understanding during the last climb was hardly a secret to people who had been watching the race on television, if only because the German had made a well-known gesture with his thumb and index finger. Aside from a few ironic comments on Ullrich's lack of discretion, the European press paid little attention to the incident. After all, it fitted fully into the structure of give-and-take that formed a fixed part of cycling tradition. When the sometime Festina team director, Bruno Roussel, described the details of the agreement in his book, however, this passage was immediately blown up into a huge bribery scandal in the United States, where cycle racing had only recently been discovered. It is obvious that, in contrast to Nestlé with its Aquarel brand, multinationals seeking to market brands globally needed to take such sensibilities into account. They could not assume that the image of their products was unaffected by reports about doping. In 1998 Coca-Cola, one of the three major sponsors of the Tour, immediately decided to reduce its investment by 80 per cent and traded its prominent position in the Tour for a much more modest one. Firms that did not withdraw in whole or in part did insist on clauses in their contracts giving them the right to cancel their obligations at once if there was another major scandal.

The sponsors' point of view was clear, of course. This time cycle racing had got off lightly and had a chance to prove itself anew. But the first months of the 1999 season were by no means reassuring. The interception of a supply of amphetamine addressed to the Mapei team led on 1 April to large-scale action by the Belgian police during the Three Days of de Panne criterium. The Parisian narcotics squad raided the veterinary surgeon Bernard Sainz, nicknamed 'Dr Mabuse', who had a number of professional riders under his care, among them the great Belgian hope Frank Vandenbroucke. The public prosecutor at Chambery ordered an inquiry into the Flanders 2000 team because they had dumped a quantity of illicit drugs on the motorway. But the biggest scandal broke around Marco Pantani, who was on the verge of winning the Giro d'Italia when, two days before the finish, he was found to have a hematocrit value – the percentage of red blood cells – well above the permitted 50 per cent and was sent home. Yet it could all have been much worse. The stream of revelations Marie-George Buffet had hoped for did not come to pass. The cycling world had closed itself off against the outside world like a fortress under siege. Riders hardly ever spoke to journalists any more, and none of the still-active professionals were willing to offer particulars about doping in the peloton. This gave UCI president Hein Verbruggen the opportunity to claim with much aplomb that Festina was 'an exceptional case'. Leblanc expressed himself in the same vein, stating that a new culture held sway in the peloton.

x x x

The Tour of 1999 was an important test case. A repeat of the events of the year before could have been fatal. The organisers and all others who were commercially associated with cycle racing no doubt held their breath for three long weeks, but everything seemed to go wonderfully well. True, the Belgian Ludo Dierckxens was suspended, but only because he had failed to give timely notice that his knee had been treated with corticoids. He did not even test positive. Moreover, this rather innocent incident was completely overshadowed by what was described in *L'Equipe* as 'the most sensational comeback in the history of sport'. Its hero was the American Lance Armstrong. In 1993, aged 21, he had become world champion. During the next three seasons he scored a number of other major victories and rose to sixth place in the world rankings. In 1996 he was diagnosed with testicular cancer, which had spread into his lungs and abdomen. His chances of survival were estimated to be no better than 50-50. After an operation and three months of intensive chemotherapy he was declared to be provisionally cured and ready to begin his recovery. Scarcely anyone reckoned with the possibility that he would be able to resume his racing career, and it seemed almost a miracle when he not only appeared at the start of the Ruta del Sol in February 1999 but also completed it. A fourth place in the Tour of Spain and a second place in the Amstel Gold Race indicated that he was nearing his earlier form, and in the absence of Ullrich and Pantani he was even thought to be one of the favourites in the 1999 Tour. Armstrong showed himself to be superior in the time trials, and with a win in the major Alpine stage he also removed all doubts about his climbing abilities, which before his illness had been only fair to middling. In Paris he had a lead of seven-and-a-half minutes over the second-placed man on general classification, the ex-Festina rider Alex Zülle, whose suspension had been lifted just in time.

The Tour had stayed completely free from scandal and had an almost ideal victor. Yet in no way could the organisers be complacent. Nothing suggested that the riders subscribed to a new mentality as Jean-Marie Leblanc had hoped. On the contrary, there were clear signs that made observers suspect the opposite. First, there was the enormously high speed at which the Tour was ridden. In 1962, the first time in 30 years that the Tour was competed for by factory teams, Anquetil set a record with an average speed of 37.32 km/h. Twenty-five years later the record, which by then was held by Hinault, was at 37.84 km/h, only slightly higher. Starting in 1988, however, the year that EPO was introduced into sport and the use of anabolic steroids had reached a peak, the speed with which the Tour was ridden went up by leaps and bounds. In 1992 it rose above 39 km/h for the first time. In 1998, the year of the Festina scandal, it actually went up to 39.98 km/h. If 1999 had really been a 'Tour of renewal', it would have been only logical for the average to drop sharply. Jean-Marie Leblanc had let it be known beforehand that he would be very pleased with an average of 37 km/h. But nothing of the kind happened; quite the contrary. Indeed, with 40.28 km/h, a new record was set. Even more disturbing were the results of the blood tests. Although none of the riders had a hematocrit value higher than the permitted 50 per cent, the average was no lower than in the 1998 Tour. The only logical inference was that the riders were using just as much EPO as the year before but had become more adept in masking it. This would later be confirmed by the mountain biker Jérôme Chiotti and the road racer Filippo Simeoni, the first two still-active professionals who broke the vow of silence towards the outside world and revealed the extent of doping in cycle racing. Both were immediately suspended by the UCI authorities, who realised all too well how dangerous this lack of discretion was.

How much doubt existed about Leblanc's assurance that the 1999 Tour was a new beginning was evident also from the very mixed reaction which greeted Armstrong's victory. Under other circumstances the comeback by the American would unquestionably have gained a place of honour in the gallery of Tour legends. But after the Festina affair and the revelations that followed it, nothing was as suspect as a miracle. Of course, Armstrong had millions of admirers, especially in the United States, who rejected with indignation all suggestions that his comeback had not come about in an entirely natural fashion. But against this there were many who asked themselves what extraordinary substances the American had used to accomplish so miraculous a feat.

The hue and cry was started by the French journal *Le Monde* with the revelation that traces of corticoids had been found in Armstrong's urine after the first stage. The American did not deny it, but according to him it was merely the result of applying ointment to his painful rear end after the prologue. Because the quantities of the banned substance were microscopically small – in contrast to what was claimed in *Le Monde* – and had, indeed, been absent at the inspection the day before, this explanation was accepted. This was not altogether according to the rules. Strictly speaking, Armstrong was allowed to use the ointment only if he had provided a doctor's note before the start of the Tour. But that the matter was blown so hugely out of proportion, with *Le Monde* quite forgetting its customary meticulousness, indicates how deeply rooted the mistrust was. The fact that in France and Italy Armstrong gained the nickname 'Robocop' – half human, half robot – points in the same direction.

It also occasions no surprise that the doubts surrounding Armstrong's victory did not end with the one corticoid incident. He and his team rarely escaped from the critical eye of the media even for a moment. Thus, reporters for the French TV channel France 3, who apparently wanted to show themselves to be every bit as inventive as their colleagues at France 2 in 1998, were able to get hold of a garbage bag used by the US Postal team and found empty containers of injection needles and medications. This led to a judicial enquiry that went on for two years but yielded no results at all. Yet this, too, did not end the steady flow of rumours. On the contrary, it received a new impulse when it became known that since 1995 Armstrong had been in contact with the Italian sports physician Michele Ferrari, regarded as one of the driving forces behind the spread of EPO in the cycling world. From that moment onwards almost everything Armstrong did or did not do prompted new suspicions. Why did he get going so late in the season? Was this perhaps because that way he could train for months without being tested? And was that also the reason why he moved from France to Spain, more relaxed where doping was concerned, so that he did not need to fear unexpected tests? Questions like this, asked over and over again, demonstrate the most important result of the anti-doping policy: a rider cannot perform an outstanding feat without immediately coming under suspicion. Of course it would be sad if Armstrong's wonderful comeback was accomplished in part by artificial means. But it would be much sadder if the American does owe his comeback solely to will power and perseverance and never gets the recognition that is his due.

The cycling journalist and historian Pierre Chany, who covered the Tour almost 50 times during his career, said just before he died in 1996 that doping would be the death of cycle sport. At the time no one paid much attention to his words, but in the meantime they seem to have become prophetic. This is all the more so because the possibility that the use of stimulants will ever disappear is minimal. The notion that a new cycling culture can quickly take form, as Jean-Marie Leblanc assumed, is pure illusion, if only because riders find themselves in a vicious circle. Because they know or in any case strongly suspect that their competitors use drugs, they feel compelled to do so as well, even when they realise they are endangering their own health. But even if the whole peloton were by some miracle or other suddenly to become clean, there would always be cyclists who would not be able to resist taking that little bit that could help them to a victory, whereupon the process would begin anew. This cannot be countered, moreover, because inspections and tests will never be adequate to the purpose. After all, new pharmaceutical products are developed more quickly than the means to detect them. To determine whether riders have them in their possession, constant home searches would have to take place, not only in the riders' houses, but in those of their entourage. But even if it were technically possible to place the entire peloton under permanent surveillance, this would offer no guarantee that doping could be eliminated. When a lot of money is at stake corruption is almost unavoidable. Ex-rider Jean-Christophe Currit revealed in 1999 that some physicians were willing to cover up a positive test in exchange for a bribe of between £4,500 and £6,000. Five years earlier he himself had been caught using amphetamine, but this never became public. To the extent that supervision becomes tighter, the trade in prohibited substances will, moreover, increasingly end up in criminal hands, with the result that doping will become even more difficult to deal with. A first indication of this development was the case of the Italian cyclist Dario Frigo. In 2001 he bought, on the black market, a product that had not even been released, and was still in an experimental stage, or at least so he believed.

x x x

Tougher measures and harsher penalties will certainly not end the use of stimulants. There is a much larger chance that the drug-hunters' attempts to clean up the sport will do irreparable damage. The negative effects of their behaviour are already greater than the positive. Alas, there is no way back. Powerful North American leagues such as the National Basketball Association and the National Hockey League are the last bastions where sportsmen may themselves decide how to prepare themselves for games. The chances that the UCI will ever join them are zero.

Even though the doping problem will probably increase rather than decrease in the coming years, this does not mean that Chany's pessimistic expectations will come true. The future of bicycle road racing does not depend in the first instance on whether stimulants are used or not. Much more important is the attitude of the public. As long as it continues to be as enthusiastic as it is now there will always be sponsors enough; and it is very unlikely the authorities will resort to Draconian measures. Marie-George Buffet did say during the Festina affair that no Tour was better than a Tour with doping, but that has not become a government policy guideline. On the contrary, it seems French Prime Minister Lionel Jospin personally restrained the minister and the hawks among the magistrates from again launching large-scale raids during the 1999 Tour. These have not taken place in subsequent Tours either, in spite of ample indications that doping is still widespread in the peloton. For example, a police raid during the 2001 Giro led to charges against 51 persons, among them 37 riders. However, it is clear that for now the French authorities have taken the line that it is politically much too hazardous to use a heavy hand against the Tour. After all, it is officially recognised as part of the national heritage. This is not just an idle designation. The Tour does occupy a place in France that for a sporting event is quite unique. Tales of riders who had to confront pain and fatigue under dreadful weather conditions or on terrible roads have a secure place in French history. In many places there are memorials that mark high points in a century of Tour history as though they were memorable feats of arms. Thus there is a monument for Henri Desgrange on the Galibier, for Jacques Goddet on the Tourmalet, for Tommy Simpson on Mont Ventoux, for Gino Bartali in Briançon, for Fausto Coppi and Louison Bobet in the Casse-Déserte of the Col d'Izoard, for René Vietto on the Col de Braus, and for René Pottier on the Ballon d'Alsace. There are plaques in Saint-Marie-de-Campan where Eugène Christophe repaired his front fork, at the descent of the Aubisque where Wim van Est crashed into a ravine, and on the Côte de Bonsecours where Jean Robic launched his decisive breakaway in 1947. Even the duel between Coppi and Jan Nolten on the Puy de Dôme has been officially memorialised since 2002.

Still, this glorification has another side. It does add to the Tour's status, but at the same time it obliges the organisers to keep bringing back something of the glories of the past. That is certainly no easy task, and Tour management generally makes no more than a couple of gestures. Cols with legendary status continue to get a high rating in the mountain classification, while every year a lot of yesterday's stars are invited. Sometimes they perform an official function, but usually they need do no more than shake hands, be recognised, and revive nostalgic memories. But that cannot alter the fact that over time the Tour de France has fundamentally changed. It began with 60 riders and just one escorting vehicle, but since then it has become so extensive a media spectacle that little can be left to improvisation. Nor is there much room for feats that can be described as 'heroic', not only because of the less demanding route and the constant assistance from team directors, technicians, and trainers, but also because the balance of power has changed. Desgrange could send his riders through the mountains along 300 kilometres of badly paved roads, in rain or in snow. That is impossible these days. Of course, cyclists were never all that keen on the conditions that were supposed to inspire them to acts of heroism, but they had no choice. That time is gone. The riders now have so much say that many of the demands they had to strike for in Hinault's time have been incorporated in the rules and regulations of the UCI. Moreover, the peloton would down tools *en masse* if the Tour management were not prepared to cancel or shorten a stage because of bad weather or icy roads, as has already happened several times. The consequence of all these changes is that it is scarcely possible any longer to perform feats that can be called 'heroic'. When the heroic element *does* appear it is mostly for reasons that in themselves have nothing to do with the progress of the race, such as Greg LeMond's comeback after his hunting accident or Lance Armstrong's after his illness. One of the rare exceptions is Marco Pantani's solo ride to Les Deux Alpes in 1998. But after this the Italian became the target of drug-hunters who pursued him with a zeal worthy of Inspector Javert in Victor Hugo's novel *Les misérables*, acting as if they wished to prevent at any price a new legend taking shape.

x x x

Not only material circumstances have given cycle road racing a wholly different look. What has also changed is an aspect that, even more than bad roads and inclement weather, constituted the essence of the 'heroic age', namely that the riders were, in principle, entirely on their own. This is scarcely true any more. Road racing is an individual sport carried on by teams, but in recent years the emphasis has increasingly been on the latter element. Team discipline in the Tour has been perfected to the point where the moments when a top rider is not surrounded by his team-mates are increasingly scarce. Sprinters usually need to get to the front no more than 200 metres before the finish, while climbers can often ride in the slipstream of their team-mates until halfway up the last col. In this respect the Saeco team led by Mario Cipollini, and Lance Armstrong's US Postal team have set new and very high standards. This has had the consequence not only that television coverage often consists of an hours-long introduction to a few exciting moments, but also that the classic image of the lonely hero, battling against the elements and a large number of opponents, has become rare in the extreme.

In many ways the classics keep the memory of the past alive better than the Tour. That is particularly true of Paris–Roubaix and the Tour of Flanders, whose cobblestones and narrow country roads conform fully to the picture that people usually have of the heroic age, and especially in the wind and rain often experienced during these spring classics. When conditions of this kind occur, the team system often melts away, with the result that just *one* day sometimes offers more drama and excitement than three weeks of the Tour de France. Moreover, the stars of these races, cyclists such as Johan Museeuw, Gilbert Duclos-Lasalle, Franco Ballerini or Andrea Tafi, match the image of the 'forced labourers of the road' far better than Armstrong, Ullrich, Joseba Beloki or the other stars of the Tour.

How much the quasi-archaic character of bicycle road racing speaks to the public is particularly evident from the huge commercial success of these two classics. During the Festina trial, Jean-Marie Leblanc announced in Lille that of the races organised by the *Société du Tour de France* only the Tour itself and Paris–Roubaix made a profit. All the other races of the STF, among them Liège–Bastogne–Liège, the Flèche Wallonne, and Paris–Tours, are annually in the red.

The success of Paris–Roubaix demonstrates clearly how much importance attaches to the past in cycle racing. Attempts have been made in the United States, Canada, Great Britain, and Japan to create races with something of a world-wide character. In spite of immediately getting the designation of 'classic' and even being included in the rankings for the World Cup instituted in 1989, within a few years they all disappeared. The German HEW-Classic Hamburg and especially the Spanish Classica San Sebastian undoubtedly enjoy better chances of survival, but the status of these races is not very high and the organisers rarely succeed in attracting many stars. Little else could be expected in a sport in which even after 40 years the Amstel Gold Race is thought of as an upstart.

The link between seniority and prestige is so close, and cycle sport is so tightly connected to the past, that it sometimes seems there is little room for rejuvenation. That is a misconception, though. Even Paris–Roubaix is much more modern than appears at first sight. Jacques Goddet saw it as 'a last remnant of the heroic past, the last link with the tradition to which cycle sport owes its greatness'. In fact, this is completely wrong. Théodore Vienne and Maurice Perez, who took the initiative in launching the first edition back in 1896, would have been extremely surprised had they known their race would some day be known as the toughest, most primitive, and most inhuman one-day race in the cycling calendar. After all, they actually did their best to create a less demanding race, freed of the heroic qualities of the monster races often conducted in those days. The most important barrier was the incline at Doullens. Its height was no more than 151 metres, but in an age without gears it was a major obstacle which only the strongest riders could conquer without having to dismount. The notorious cobblestones did not play a significant role, and they were hardly even mentioned in the newspaper accounts. In fixing the route, Victor Breyer, the editor of *Paris-Vélo*, had even tried to avoid them as much as possible. The 'Belgian blocks', as they were called at the time, were to be found only during the last 30 kilometres, but they did not present much of a problem because the cyclists were allowed to make ample use of the pavements. Breyer would also have been shocked by the idea of leading the riders along the passage through the Wallers-Aremberg Woods. The stretches of cobblestones that are now included in the route are grimmer and more primitive than the roads along which cyclists had to ride a century ago. Today's Paris–Roubaix is a reconstruction of a past that has never existed. The same thing applies to the Tour of Flanders and its many 'bergskes' – little mountains. These too, were only later made part of the route. The most 'legendary' passage in the Tour of Flanders, the ascent of the Kapelmuur in Gerardsbergen, was adopted into the route as recently as 1981.

That the two most successful classics of the present era owe their reputation largely to an illusion is not a negative but in fact a very positive point. What has made bicycle road racing so unique – from the races in Saint-Cloud in 1868 to the present day – has never been its actual history but always its mythical portrait. That is the reason, too, why it continues to renew itself today without losing its special character. In scarcely any other sport does tradition seem to play a more important role. But that tradition is by no means fixed. On the contrary, it is constantly being reinvented.

Index of Names